THE COMPARATION OF A VYRGIN AND A MARTYR

The Comparation

of

A Vyrgin and a Martyr

(1523)

by

Desiderius Erasmus

Translated

by

Thomas Paynell

A Facsimile Reproduction
of the Berthelet Edition of 1537
with an Introduction

by

William James Hirten

Gainesville, Florida
Scholars' Facsimiles & Reprints
1970

SCHOLARS' FACSIMILES & REPRINTS

1605 N.W. 14TH AVENUE

GAINESVILLE, FLORIDA, 32601, U.S.A.

HARRY R. WARFEL, GENERAL EDITOR

L.C. CATALOG CARD NUMBER: 70-101148

SBN 8201-1072-8

Manufactured in the U.S.A.

INTRODUCTION

During the years 1521-1529 Erasmus made his residence at Basel. This period is naturally viewed by Erasmian scholars as one of stormy disputes and significant publications. They remember the *Spongia,* a result of Ulrich von Hutten's visit to the city and his unsuccessful attempt to obtain an interview with Erasmus. They again become a-ware not only of *De Libero Arbitrio* and the religious conflict with Luther but also of the *Ciceronianus* and the literary controversy with over-enthusiastic Latin classicists. And they recall the *Christiani Matrimonii Institutio* and the enlarged edition of the *Colloquia,* as well as those editions, printed by John Froben, of various Church Fathers.

But they tend to overlook a short composition written during these troublesome and yet relatively productive years in the career of the great humanist—a work which exudes peace and which apparently was written in a spirit free from contention and strife, either literary or theological. The recipients of this treatise were religious women. The cause of writing was the desire to thank them for a gift; the purpose, a spirit that would lead to devotion, "ad pietatem."

Erasmus mentions this work, *Virginis et Martyris Comparatio,* in the letter to John Botzheim known as the *Catalogus Lucubrationum,* stating

that he had composed the treatise at the request
of a certain Helias, director of a religious community at Cologne: "ad preces integerrimi viri
Heliae. . . ."[1] Later in the *Catalogus* Erasmus
groups some of his works which he believes
should direct the reader in the ways of piety, including among them the *Enchiridion*, the *Paracle-
sis, De Immensa Dei Misericordia Concio*, and
"Comparatio virginitatis et martyrii, ad virgines
Colonienses."[2]

This last mentioned work began as a letter,
dated 1523, written by Erasmus to the Benedic-
tine nuns of the Convent of the Machabees, Cologne.[3] These religious women had sent him a
gift of confectionery, and he wrote to thank them
for the "xeniis quae delectant palatum."[4] This
letter, it has been suggested, may therefore be a
reply to thank the recipients for a *strena*, or New
Year's gift, and it is further proposed that the
opening words indicate a similar *strena* of confections sent by the nuns to Erasmus for the previous New Year also.[5] But the nuns had appar-

---

[1]*Opvs Epistolarvm Des. Erasmi Roterodami*, ed. by
P. S. Allen, H. M. Allen, and H. W. Garrod (Oxford,
1906-1947), i, 21 (ep. I). Although it bears the earlier
date, this is not the original letter but rather a revision
of it made by Erasmus and published by Froben, September, 1524; see the commentary, p. 1, as well as the
commentary on ep. 1474 (v, 509). This edition of Erasmus's letters will be subsequently cited as Allen.

[2]Allen, i, 40 (ep. I).

[3]*Ibid.*, v, 236 (ep. 1346); the salutation is to the
"Collegio Virginvm Macabeiticarvm apvd Coloniam
Agrippinam."

[4]Allen, v, 237 (ep. 1346).

[5]*Ibid.*, v, 236 (commentary on ep. 1346). The letter
begins, "Semel atque iterum tragematis ac dulciariis
missis prouocat me pietas vestra, virgines optimae, . . ."

ently expressed the hope that Erasmus might re-
ciprocate by conveying to them some sentiments
of spiritual delectation, "ea quae pascant ani-
mum,"[6] and this letter of response ran, in an
early published edition, about seven pages.[7] The
date given at the end is merely the year, "Anno
salutiferae Incarnationis M.D.XXIII."[8]

This letter was published within the same year,
though not independently. In the *Catalogus* Erasmus speaks of his recension of the *Ratio Verae
Theologiae,* and in the same document he placed
this "Methodus verae theologiae" among those of
his works conducive to piety.[9] The revised *Ratio*
was printed at Cologne by Alopecius in the De-
cember of 1523; there was also an undated edition, without place, which may have been printed
in Basel for Michael Hillen, publisher of Antwerp.
At the end of each of these editions is the letter
Erasmus addressed to the Cologne community.[10]

This letter was not to remain the final and
definitive text of *Virginis et Martyris Comparatio.*
Within the following year Erasmus wrote an
expanded text, apparently at the request of Helias Marcaeus, the director of the same convent

---

[6]Allen, v, 237 (ep. 1346).

[7]It will be noted that only the introductory and final
passages of the work are reprinted in Allen (see v, 236,
commentary on ep. 1346).

[8]Allen, v, 237 (ep. 1346).

[9]*Ibid.,* i, 21, 40 (ep. I).

[10]These editions are treated in Allen, v, 285-286
(commentary on ep. 1365). See also *Bibliotheca Erasmiana: Répertoire des Oeuvres d'Érasme* (Nieuwkoop,
1961), 1st Series, p. 168. The introductory and final
passages of the letter reprinted in Allen are based on
the undated edition of the *Ratio* (see Allen, v, commentaries on pp. 236, 286).

for which he had written the original letter. This enlarged text, now actually a treatise, was, like the original letter, not published independently but was appended to the *De Immensa Dei Misericordia Concio*, another treatise which Erasmus viewed as a pious undertaking. This latter work, with *Virginis et Martyris Comparatio*, was published in many editions, among them being those of Strassburg (1523, Knoblouch), Antwerp (1524, Hillen), and Basel (September, 1524, Froben).[11] Furthermore, *Virginis et Martyris Comparatio* was included in an edition of *De Pueris Instituendis* (Basel, 1529, Jerome Froben, Herwagen, and Episcopius)[12] and, before the close of the century, was translated into German, Italian, and English ("The Comparation of a Vyrgin and a Martyr"). There were later renderings into Dutch and French and an undated translation into Flemish.[13]

In the Froben edition of *Virginis et Martyris Comparatio* previously mentioned, that of Basel, September, 1524, there was a short preface by Erasmus dated July 30, 1524, at Basel, and addressed to Helias Marcaeus, director of the Cologne convent.[14] In these few introductory remarks Erasmus assures his correspondent that he

---

[11]*Bibliotheca Erasmiana*, 1st Series, pp. 180-181. See also Allen, vol. v, commentaries on epistles 1346 (p. 236) and 1474, 1475 (p. 509).

[12]*Bibliotheca Erasmiana*, 1st Series, p. 180; Allen, commentaries on epistles 603 (iii, 14) and 1346 (v, 236).

[13]*Bibliotheca Erasmiana*, 1st Series, p. 181.

[14]See preface to *Virginis et Martyris Comparatio*, in *Omnia Opera Des. Erasmi* (Basel: Froben, 1540), v, 492; this edition of Erasmus's works will be subsequently cited as *Opera Erasmi*. See also Allen, v, 509-510 (ep. 1475, with commentary).

is sending the treatise, a "libellum," and begs his indulgence for both its brevity and tardiness, advancing as an excuse the great number of activities which keep him occupied, such as the sending and receiving of letters. He concludes with an expression of esteem for the religious of the convent and for their director, the "vir optime."[15]

This Convent of the Machabees was named in honor of the seven brothers and their mother, all martyrs, the story of whose death, in about 168 B.C., is narrated in the second Book of Machabees. These martyrs were also cited in the writings of various Church Fathers,[16] and Erasmus, as might be expected, praised their courage in his *Virginis et Martyris Comparatio*.[17] According to tradition, relics of these martyrs were honored in Antioch in the fourth century, some of the relics were brought to Constantinople about two hundred years later, and some are now in the church of San Pietro in Vincoli in Rome. Also, according to a further tradition, some of the relics were brought to Cologne about the twelfth century and were subsequently placed in the Convent of the

---

[15]This short introductory epistle is not rendered in the English translation of 1537, which is given in facsimile in this volume. An English version of the epistle, translated by the editor, precedes the facsimile text.

[16]The account of the seven brothers, their mother, and the scribe Eleazar is found in 2 Machabees, VI, 18-31; VII, 1-41. See also *Butler's Lives of the Saints*, ed. by Herbert Thurston, S.J., and Donald Attwater (New York, 1956), iii, 237-238; H. Bévenot, "Makkabäische Brüder," *Lexikon für Theologie und Kirche*, vi (1934), col. 818.

[17]*Opera Erasmi*, v, 497; see Erasmus, *The Comparation*, Paynell translation, pp. 42-46 of this book.

Machabees.[18] This convent, a community of Bene-
dictine nuns, was founded about the year 1178.[19]
It might be of some interest to note that about
three centuries later, in the mid fifteenth century,
when Johannes Busch and Nicholas of Cusa were
attempting to correct monastic abuses, the Convent of the Machabees apparently seemed willing
to enter into the spirit of reform.[20]

Helias Marcaeus, the director of the community
at the time when Erasmus wrote the *Virginis et
Martyris Comparatio,* was native of Jülich. He
was a theologian and probably father confessor to
the nuns, to whom he was also a generous bene-
factor. It was he who donated to the convent the
reliquary for the Machabean relics.[21] He extended
his interest in the Machabean martyrs to the do-
main of letters; and persuaded Erasmus, probably
about the year 1518, to revise a Latin text of a
work, attributed to Flavius Josephus, entitled *Peri
autokratoros logismou.*[22]

---

[18]Bévenot, col. 818; Allen, iii, 310 (commentary on
ep. 842), accepts Archbishop Reinold Dassel, who died
in 1167, as the one who brought the relics from Italy.

[19]R. Haass, "Kirchen u. Klöster," in section on
"Köln," *Lexikon für Theologie und Kirche,* vi (1961),
col. 388.

[20]Dom Philibert Schmitz, *Histoire de l'Ordre de
Saint-Benoît,* vol. VII: *Les Moniales* (1956, Éditions de
Maredsous), p. 112. "Parmi les abbayes qui reprirent
l'observance régulière dans la seconde moitié du XVᵉ
siècle, citons Saint-Maurice et les Machabées à Cologne,
. . ."

[21]J. J. Merlo in *Allgemeine Deutsche Biographie s.v.*
"Marcäus: Helias," xx (1884), 294. This article further
states that the reliquary was to be found in more recent
times in the Andreaskirche, also in Cologne; see Bévenot, col. 818.

[22]Allen, iii, 310-311 (commentary on ep. 842).

This narrative, which treats of the heroism of
the seven brothers and their mother, is mentioned by Eusebius of Caesarea in his *Historia
Ecclesiastica* as one of the works of the celebrated
Jewish historian.[23] Erasmus seemed willing to review the text and make corrections. An edition
subsequently appeared, without date: *"Peri autokratoros logismou*, hoc est de Imperatrice ratione
. . . a D. Erasmo Roterodamo, diligenter recognitus
et emendatus."* It was printed at Cologne by Cer-
vicornus.[24] The date of publication can be con-
jectured from a letter, included with the text, addressed to Helias Marcaeus from a Dominican of
Cologne, Father Magdalius Iacobus Gaudensis,
and dated June 5, 1517. Professor Allen proposed
that Erasmus may have done his revision during
the year following, since he had passed through
Cologne during the May of 1518.[25]

This edition also included a communication by
Erasmus, addressed to Helias, "pater integer-
rime," which served as a preface to the text at-

---

[23]*Historia Ecclesiastica*, book iii, ch. X; see J.-P.
Migne, *Patrologia Graeca*, xx (1857), cols. 243-244.

[24]*Catalogue Général des Livres Imprimés de la Bib-
liothèque Nationale*, lxxviii (1931), col. 1280, no. 149;
Bibliotheca Erasmiana, 2nd Series, p. 37; *British Museum
General Catalogue of Printed Books*: Photolithographic
Edition to 1955, cxix (1962), col. 265.

[25]Allen, iii, 310-311 (commentary on ep. 842); this
date is supported by the epistle of Peter Gilles, ep. 846
and commentary (iii, 339-340). This edition *Peri autokratoros logismou* should not be confused with Josephus's *Bellum Iudaicum*, the manuscript of which Erasmus attempted to obtain for Jerome Froben and thus
became involved in correspondence with George d'Ar-
magnac, John de Pins, and Rabelais: see Allen, ix, 380-
382, 469-470 (eps. 2569, 2628, with commentaries); x,
130 (ep. 2743).

tributed to Josephus. In this preface Erasmus
confesses that he spent very little time in his re-
vising and that he had no Greek codex from
which to do his work. He then proceeds to be-
stow high praise on the eloquence of Josephus,
stating that St. Jerome held this little work of
the historian in great esteem for its style of
writing.[26] Erasmus concludes by congratulating
the Convent of the Machabees and all of Cologne on the possession of very precious relics, ex-
pressing the hope that the lives of those whose
relics are thus honored will inspire the people of
the city in the practice of virtue.[27]

About three years after the publication of
Virginis et Martyris Comparatio Erasmus speaks
of the death of Helias Marcaeus. In a letter to
Tielmann Gravius,[28] dated Basel, August 27, 1527,
he laments that this good old man has been taken
from this world but rejoices that he has gone to
a better one: "Heliam optimum senem nobis erep-

---

[26]It has now been accepted by many that this narrative, referred to by Eusebius as the *Makkabaïkon*, which
treats of the martyrdom of the seven brothers and their
mother, should not be attributed to Josephus. See
Eusebius, *Church History*, in vol. i of *A Select Library
of Nicene and Post-Nicene Fathers of the Christian
Church*, 2nd Series, ed. by Philip Schaff and Henry Wace
(New York, 1890), p. 145, n. 6; the translation, with
notes, is by Rev. Arthur Cushman McGiffert. See also
"Introduction" to *Josephus*, vol. i (London and New
York, 1926), p. xii, tr. by H. St. J. Thackeray (Loeb
Classical Library). The reference by St. Jerome is found
in his *Liber de Viris Illustribus*, Ch. XIII; see J.-P.
Migne, *Patrologia Latina*, xxiii (1883), cols. 661-662.

[27]Allen, iii, 311-312 (ep. 842); a German translation
of this preface can be found in *Erasmus von Rotterdam
Briefe*, ed. by Walther Köhler (Wiesbaden, 1947), pp.
193-194 (ep. 127).

[28]Allen, vii, 151-152 (ep. 1865).

tum doleo, coelis redditum gaudeo." He states
that, in his correspondence, he had to offer Helias
a friendly rebuke because the latter in his final
letters seemed to sense the imminence of his own
end. Erasmus then implies that Helias was pre-
vented from answering by his death: "Respondit
ille non calamo sed re."[29]

Thus one looking in retrospect at *Virginis et
Martyris Comparatio* can see it arising from a
background not of strife and controversy but of
peace and friendly association. The reader may
conclude, if he judges from the many editions that
appeared, including translations into other lan-
guages, that the treatise retained a certain popu-
larity during the sixteenth century.[30]

THE WORK OF ERASMUS

A careful perusal of *Virginis et Martyris Comparatio* should convince the reader that Erasmus,
in composing this work, demonstrated a keen
sense of order and a mastery of literary form.
Although the work is composed as an extended
letter or a treatise, it seems to fit the logical pattern proposed by Cicero for oratorical persua-
sion,[31] as a synopsis of the entire treatise would
seem to suggest.

Erasmus begins by contrasting the pleasant
confections which the nuns have sent him with
the spiritual nourishment which he has been re-

---

[29]*Ibid.*, vii, 152 (ep. 1865).

[30]*Bibliotheca Erasmiana*, 1st Series, pp. 180-181.

[31]The *Moriae Encomium*, which Erasmus wrote in the
form of an oration, fits this pattern very well, as is shown
most convincingly by Hoyt H. Hudson in the introduction
to his edition of *The Praise of Folly* (Princeton, 1941), pp.
xiv-xvi, 129-142.

quested to give in return. He compliments these religious women on their desire for spiritual reading but modestly regrets that they have sought it from so unsatisfactory a source as himself.

He then reminds his readers that the consecrated virgin has, in a spiritual sense, a divine spouse, Christ, Who showed Himself greater in redeeming the world than in creating it. In a special way Christ is the glory of martyrs and virgins; He is their strength and model as well. Very appropriately the author introduces the two flower symbols: the rose of martyrdom and the lily of virginity. Although matrimony, he asserts, is an honorable state, only too often must a worthy wife submit to the tribulations inflicted by an unworthy husband; in contrast, the woman consecrated to virginity, being liberated from worldly concerns, can devote her time in the direct service of the Lord.

The following section of the treatise is inspired by a liturgical hymn, the first line of which reads "Jesu, corona virginum."[32] Erasmus quotes each of the four stanzas separately, providing a short commentary after each one.[33] In these re-

---

[32]This hymn, of four stanzas, is found in the office of Vespers for the common feast of virgins; see *The Liber Usualis*, with Int. and Rubrics in English, ed. by the Benedictines of Solesmes (New York, 1938), pp. 1211-1214. Migne, in *Patrologia Latina*, xvii (1879), col. 1259, no. LXXX ("De Virginibus"), gives two versions of the hymn, placing them among hymns attributed to St. Ambrose; the second version corresponds to the text previously referred to in the *Liber Usualis*.

[33]The version of the hymn employed by Erasmus differs from those in the *Liber Usualis* and in Migne (see previous footnote). However, the variations in all three versions do not seem to differ essentially.

JESU, CORONA VIRGINUM*

Iesu corona uirginum,
quem mater illa concipit,
quae sola uirgo parturit,
haec uota clemens accipe.

Qui pascis inter lilia
septus coronis uirginum,
sponsas decorans gloria,
sponsisque reddens praemia.

Quocumque pergis, uirgines
sequuntur, atque laudibus
post te canentes cursitant,
hymnosque dulces personant.

Te depecamur largius,
nostris adauge mentibus,
nescire prorsus omnia
corruptionis uulnera.

---

*The version of the liturgical hymn quoted in *Virginis et Martyris Comparatio*: see *Opera Erasmi*, v, 494 (lines 35-36, 42-43), 495 (lines 7-8), 495 (line 54)-496 (line 1); Paynell tr., p. 17, lines 7-11 and line 20 to line 4 on p. 18; p. 21, lines 4-8; p. 28, lines 18-21. Erasmus provides a commentary after each stanza. Also see footnotes 32 and 33.

flections he states that since the consecrated virgin is the spouse of Christ, the faithful shepherd of the flock, He will grant the great reward of everlasting beatitude. The virgin, in turn, is expected to show fidelity to Christ, even to following Him to His passion and death. She must be free of all false doctrine,[34] all unchastity in thought, and such sins as envy, arrogance, and backbiting. Unlike the married woman, she is not distracted by and burdened with worldly cares; and to emphasize the virgin's complete commitment to the service of her Lord, Erasmus employs the figure of the dove, a symbol prominent in the *Canticum Canticorum* of the Scriptures.

Returning to the symbols of the rose and the lily, Erasmus lays stress on the great honor in which the Church has always held martyrs and virgins: those who "wyllyngly and gladly offred theyr bodies to be cruelly turmented" and those who "wyllyngly for the kyngdome of god gaue them selfe [w]holly to lyue chaste."[35] Their heroic virtue has so inspired Christian writers that, in celebrating the glories of martyrs and virgins, Prudentius has soared higher than Pindar and Horace, and so also have Church Fathers like John Chrysostom, Cyprian, and Ambrose written

---

[34]"Iam uirginitas uera non tantum sita est in dono castitatis, sed omne animi uitium huius uirginitatis est corruptio. Qui deflexit a rectitudine fidei catholicae, huius contaminata est uirginitas": *Opera Erasmi*, v, 496 (lines 6-8). The Paynell tr., p. 29, reads "Nor trewe virginitie resteth not only in the gyft of chastitie, but all vyce of the mynde is the corruption of this virginitie. Who soo euer swarueth from the true feyth catholyke, his virginitie is defiled."

[35]*Opera Erasmi*, v, 496 (lines 34-36) ; Paynell tr., p. 34.

with a style surpassing that of Cicero.[36] Martyrs
indeed are justly honored after their heroic
deaths, but virgins receive honor during their life-
time. This respect for virginity is rendered even
by the barbarian and by the enemy in time of war.
Early Christian writers such as Tertullian and St.
Jerome were almost excessive in extolling virginity, but, Erasmus adds, such praise should not be
construed in any way derogatory to the married
state.

Erasmus concludes this section of the work by
recalling to his readers' minds the heroic example
of the Machabean martyrs. The mother, although
she had through parenthood surrendered her virginity, still in a sense restored it, according to
the author, "with the martyrdome of so many
sonnes vyrgyns."[37] Furthermore, her martyrdom
was greater than theirs because she had to wit-
ness the cruel torments of her children and also,
as a beholder, suffer their deaths before under-
going her own. Thus Erasmus insists that these
seven youths anticipated the practice of Christian
virtues, and he cites Scriptural passages in which
Our Lord counsels virginity religiously motivated
and the acceptance of the cross. He further comments how fitting it is that relics of the Machabean martyrs should be treasured at the Convent
of the Machabees, "a holy college of virgins."[38]

At this point Erasmus inquires as to which is
the greater, martyrdom or virginity. Aptly rein-

---

[36]*Opera Erasmi*, v, 496 (lines 48-53); Paynell tr., pp.
36-37. With these Church Fathers, Paynell mentions
also St. Jerome ("Hieronymus").

[37]Paynell tr., p. 42; *Opera Erasmi*, v. 497 (lines 27-
28).

[38]Paynell tr., p. 46; *Opera Erasmi*, v, 497 (line 47).

troducing the flower symbols, he declares that
when the rose and the lily are mingled in the
same basket, the beauty of one serves the
splendor of the other. However, in making his
comparison, he tends to give the palm to virginity,[39] without in any way lessening the glory of
martyrdom. It is necessary for some, he says, to
suffer death for their faith, but virginity is freely
offered. If martyrs should again be required, they
would most likely be found in the ranks of virgins,
who daily conduct a constant warfare of the spirit
against worldly enticements. Some of the greatest
martyrs were virgin saints such as Agnes, Cecelia,
and Agatha. Although martyrs and virgins, both
in their own way exemplify victory over the
flesh: martyrdom flourishes after death, but virginity develops and thrives during life. Indeed,
the commitment of religious virginity is above
human power and assumes a dignity comparable
to the angelic.

Having thus far written so glowingly of virginity, Erasmus next warns his readers that this
state of life must be lived in the spirit of total
consecration to Christ. A virgin must be chaste
in mind as well as in deed, she must not dress
in brilliant and costly apparel, and her adornment must be not worldly but spiritual. Her
defence against mundane attractions lies in
prayer, fasting, spiritual reading, and pious
works, such as charity in helping the poor and the
needy. Her conversing with a young man of the

---

[39]This is the interpretation of Ephraim Emerton, *Desiderius Erasmus of Rotterdam* (New York and London,
1899), p. 436.

world is like talking to the serpent, who caused
the downfall of Eve; rather, the virgin should imitate Mary, who spoke to an angel sent from
heaven: "Ecce ancilla domini."[40] The outward
and showy pleasures of worldly virgins fade after
youth, but the inward joys of the virgin consecrated to her Lord abide into eternity. The married woman is frequently saddened and oppressed
by an unworthy husband, but the true virgin is
espoused to Christ, Who freely accepted humiliation and suffering and Who requires a loving service whereby a cloister becomes not a prison but
a paradise.

In concluding the treatise, Erasmus reminds
his readers that virgins experience a spiritual
happiness expressed in their hymns and in the
recitation of the Psalms and that, above all, they
have in Christ the source of all joy and greatness.
These nuns of Cologne, he says, should imitate
the Machabean martyrs by despising the false
values of the world rather than displease God.
He ends piously, with a clause very similar to the
conclusion of a formal liturgical prayer:

> ... eritis & gloriae consortes opitulante
> sponso uestro Iesu, qui cum patre & spir-
> itu sancto uiuit & regnat in aeternum,
> Amen.[41]

> ... you shall be part takers of theyr
> glory, by the helpe of your spouse Christ
> Jesu, whiche with the father and the

---

[40]Paynell tr., pp. 57, 62-63, 65; *Opera Erasmi*, v, 499
(lines 2-4, 30-35, 48-49).

[41]*Opera Erasmi*, v, 500 (end of treatise).

holy gooste lyueth and reygneth eternally. Amen.[42]

In reading the *Virginis et Martyris Comparatio,* one becomes aware of both an orderly procession of ideas and a sense of form. A brief outline shows that the work could be fitted to the classical pattern.[43] (The Arabic numerals are used to designate the pagination of this facsimile edition.)

Exordium, 3-4
    Gratitude for a gift, 3
    Humility in accepting a new task, 4
Narratio, 5-13
    Dignity of martyrdom and of virginity, 5-9
    Symbol'sm of the rose and of the lily, 10-13
Divisio, 13-17
    Difficulties of matrimony, 13-14
    Contrast of matrimony to virginity, 14-17
Confirmatio, 17-46
    Glories of virginity (hymn attributed to St.
        Ambrose), 17-32
        (Symbolism of the dove, 25-28)
    Praise of martyrs and virgins, 32-42
        (Symbolism of the rose and of the lily, 32-
        36)

---

[42]Paynell tr., p. 77.

[43]The principal sections of the classical oration are mentioned by Cicero in bk. i, XIV (No. 19), of *De Inventione Rhetorica*: "Eae partes sex esse omnino nobis videntur: Exordium, Narratio, Partitio, Confirmatio, Reprehensio, Conclusio." The same sections, two of them with different names, are listed in a work probably erroneously attributed to Cicero: see *Rhetorica ad Herennium,* tr. by Harry Caplan (London and Cambridge, Mass., 1954, in the Loeb Classical Library), bk. i, sec. III, pp. 8-11.

One can thus maintain with good reason that
Erasmus molded his *Virginis et Martyris Comparatio* into the form employed by classic Latin
rhetoricians. That the matter of the treatise is
basically and deeply religious is almost impossible
to deny. The author sets the tone of the work by
an abundance of references and quotations from
the Scriptures. The symbols of the lily[44] and the
dove[45] are illustrated by citations from the *Canti-*

---

[44]Cant. II, 1, 2, 16-17; Cant. VI, 1; Ecclus. XXXIX,
19 (in *Opera Erasmi*, v, 494, the marginal reference is
merely *"Eccles.* 19").

[45]Cant. II, 10-12, 14; Cant. IV, 1. This last citation
is incorrectly given in the margin of the Paynell tr. as
Can. II; see p. 26, opposite line 21.

cum Canticorum and Ecclesiasticus. The asser-
tion that virgins genuinely committed to the service of Christ not only experience true joy but also
live in a noble state is supported by quotations
from both the Old and New Testaments.[46] As one
might expect, Erasmus refers to the statement in
which Our Lord consels religious virginity[47] as
well as to the section of the epistle where St. Paul
discusses marriage and celibacy.[48] Furthermore,
Erasmus uses Scriptural citations which proclaim
the glory of Christ[49] and praise Him as creator of
the world,[50] cornerstone of the Church,[51] and shepherd of souls.[52] The devotion and humility of the
Blessed Virgin are illustrated by passages from
the gospel according to St. Luke.[53] Numerous ex-
cerpts from the Bible are offered to emphasize the
abiding joy found in following Christ[54] as well as
to indicate the lot of suffering and humiliation
which invariably befalls those who wish to be true
disciples.[55] Warning the reader against tempta-

---

[46]Prov. VIII, 31; Cant. I, 7, 11; Apoc. XIV, 3-4; 2
Cor. II, 14-15. This last citation is in the Paynell tr. on
p. 72.
[47]Matt. XIX, 12.
[48]1 Cor. VII, 28-34.
[49]Ps. XLIV, 3. This reference is in the Paynell tr.
on p. 5.
[50]The Berthelet edition gives the reference as Gen. I.
Opera Erasmi, v, 493, lines 17-21 of the text, has no
marginal gloss for this comment.
[51]Acts IV, 11.
[52]John X, 11-16. This is in the Paynell tr. on p. 18.
[53]Luke I, 38, 48. See *Opera Erasmi*, v, 495, line 36;
Paynell tr., p. 25.
[54]Ps. CXIX, 5; Ps. CXXXVI, 1; Cant. I, 3; Mark XIV,
3-9; John VI, 69; Phil. I, 23; Rom. VII, 24 (*Opera
Erasmi*, v, 495, incorrectly cites Rom. VIII).
[55]Matt. XVI, 24 and Mark VIII, 34 (*Opera Erasmi*,

tions, the author cites the examples of Eve,[56] Dina,[57] and the five foolish virgins,[58] and recalls St. Paul's exhortation to guard against the allurements of evil;[59] for just as there are both true and unworthy widows,[60] so there are virgins who do not live according to the dignity of their state.

Although it is clear that Erasmus, in writing this treatise, receives his principal inspiration from the Scriptures, one might also expect that some of his ideas would be derived, at least in part, from his beloved Church Fathers. He mentions four of them: Cyprian, Ambrose, Jerome, and John Chrysostom, as well as Tertullian and the poet Prudentius; and it would be appropriate to indicate, if but briefly, a few works which these early Christian writers composed on the subjects of martyrdom and religious virginity.

St. Cyprian, in his *Epistola ad Fortunatum de Exhortatione Martyrii,* recounts the heroic deaths of the Machabean martyrs, both the seven

---

v, 497, lines 43-44); Phil. II, 6-8. This last citation is incorrectly given in the Berthelet edition as Phil. I on p. 70; see *Opera Erasmi,* v, 500, lines 16-17. Even the Machabean martyrs are hailed as "flosculi bellissimi ecclesiae . . . praecoces deliciae" ("moste fayre lyttell floures of the churche . . . rype delycacyes before your tyme"). See *Opera Erasmi,* v, 497, line 40; Paynell tr., p. 45. The account of the martyrdom is found in 2 Mac. VII, 1-41.

[56]Gen. III. See Paynell tr., pp. 57-58.

[57]Gen. XXXIV. See Paynell tr., p. 71.

[58]Matt. XXV, 1-13. See *Opera Erasmi,* v, 498, lines 49-50; Paynell tr., p. 56. Immediately after this brief comment on the five foolish virgins, Erasmus cites the "uirgines squalidas" referred to in the *Threni* or Lamentations, I, 4.

[59]2 Cor. XI, 2-3. This citation is incorrectly given in the Froben edition as 2 Cor. XII (v, 496, line 9).

[60]1 Tim. V, 3-13.

brothers and their noble mother.[61] The same
Church Father, in his *Liber de Habitu Virginum*,
warns virgins against the snares of wealth and
against excessive adornment in clothing and
jewels.[62] He quotes some Scriptural passages referred to by Erasmus in *Virginis et Martyris
Comparatio*.

St. Ambrose is the author of many works on
the subject of virginity. One of these, *De Virginibus ad Marcellinam Sororem Suam*,[63] contains
thoughts and examples later found in the treatise
of Erasmus. In extolling virginity, St. Ambrose
frequently quotes the *Canticum Canticorum*. He
speaks of the difficulties often encountered by
women in marriage and warns against worldli-
ness and unnecessary and expensive adornment.[64]
He declares the life of the Virgin Mary to be the
model for virgins, "ut ejus unius vita omnium sit
disciplina,"[65] and praises St. Agnes, who is mentioned by Erasmus, for having won the crowns of

---

[61]Migne, *Patrologia Latina*, iv (1891), cols. 694-698;
an English translation by Roy J. Deferrari is found in
Saint Cyprian: Treatises, vol. xxxvi of The Fathers of
the Church (New York, 1958), pp. 334-338.

[62]Migne, *Patrologia Latina*, iv, cols. 451-478; a translation by Sister Angela Elizabeth Keenan, S.N.D., is
found in *Saint Cyprian: Treatises*, pp. 31-52.

[63]Migne, *Patrologia Latina*, xvi (1880), cols. 197-
244. An English translation, by the Rev. H. de Romestin
et al., is found in *Nicene and Post-Nicene Fathers*, 2nd
Series, x (1896), 363-387.

[64]*De Virginibus*, in Migne, *Patrologia Latina*, xvi,
bk. i, ch. VI, cols. 206-208; and bk. iii, chs. III and VI,
cols. 234-236, 239-241. English trans., *Nicene and Post-
Nicene Fathers*, 2nd Series, x, 367-368, 382-383, 385-386.

[65]*De Virginibus*, in Migne, *Patrologia Latina*, xvi,
bk. ii, ch. II, col. 222; English trans., *Nicene and Post-
Nicene Fathers*, 2nd Series, x, 375.

both virginity and martyrdom.[66]   Also, it might
be added that in a short treatise which has been
attributed to St. Ambrose, *Ad Virginem Devotam,*
one finds the admonition to think upon the courage of the Machabean martyrs, mother and sons.[67]

Two works of St. John Chrysostom, both of
which treat of matters later discussed by Erasmus in *Virginis et Martyris Comparatio,* may be
considered briefly.   In *De Virginitate,*[68] the celebrated Greek Father speaks at length of the glory
of religious virginity but at the same time se-
verely castigates those who take a derogatory
view of marriage.   Nevertheless, the latter state,
he warns, is not without its difficulties and tribulations.   But if there are ill-advised critics of
matrimony, there are also, he further admonishes,
those who harbor an erroneous concept of virginity and who can thus be likened to the five
foolish virgins of the Scriptural parable.[69]   In
three homilies under the title *In Sanctos Maccabaeos,* St. John Chrysostom writes in praise of the
Machabean martyrs later extolled by Erasmus,
lauding especially the mother and the youngest
brother.[70]   The mother, he says, underwent

----

[66]*De Virginibus,* in Migne, *Patrologia Latina,* xvi,
bk. i, ch. II, cols. 200-202; English trans., *Nicene and
Post-Nicene Fathers,* 2nd Series, x, 364-365.

[67]Migne, *Patrologia Latina,* xvii, col. 604.

[68]*De Virginitate, Peri Parthenias,* in J.-P. Migne,
Patrologia Graeca, xlviii (1862), cols. 533-596.

[69]Matt. XXV, 1-13.   See Migne, *Patrologia Graeca,*
xlviii, col. 590 (no. LXXVII or OZ).

[70]*In Sanctos Maccabaeos, Eis tous hagious Makka-
baious* in Migne, *Patrologia Graeca,* L (1862), cols. 617-
628.   There is doubt as to St. John Chrysostom's authorship of the third homily, which praises the fortitude of
the old scribe Eleazar (see 2 Mac. VI, 18-31).

martyrdom in each of her children;[71] and Erasmus, in speaking of this very incident, would
later remind his readers that "the parentes are
more cruelly tourmented in the persecutynge of
their chylderne than in theym selfe."[72]

A few works of Tertullian may be cited to
show the esteem in which this early apologist held
both virgins and those willing to suffer martyrdom.   Accordingly, the Christian suffering for
his faith and wishing to win an incorruptible
crown looks upon the prison where he is confined
as a palaestra, a training ground.[73]   As for virgins, Tertullian, in *De Oratione,* respectfully rec-
ognizes the existence of such women who have
made a religious consecration of themselves to
Christ, and exhorts them for the sake of virtue
and modesty to cover their heads.[74]   The same
author, in both sections of *De Cultu Feminarum,*
admonishes his feminine readers to discard the
adornment of jewels, precious metals, and ornate

---

[71]Migne, *Patrologia Graeca,* L, col. 622; ". . . in singu-
lis eorum martyrium subiit, . . ."

[72]Paynell tr., p. 44; *Opera Erasmi,* v, 497 (lines 34-
35).

[73]Tertullian, *Ad Martyras,* ed. by E. Dekkers, in
Corpus Christianorum, Series Latina i (Turnhout, 1954),
6, lines 5-9.   An English translation, by Rudolph Arbes-
mann, O.S.A., is found in *Tertullian: Disciplinary, Moral
and Ascetical Works,* The Fathers of the Church, xl
(1959), 23.   The Scriptural reference is from 1 Cor. IX,
25.

[74]*De Oratione,* ed. by G. F. Diercks, in *Corpus Christianorum,* Series Latina, i, 270-271 (no. 9).   An English
translation, by Alexander Souter, is found in *Tertullian's
Treatises: Concerning Prayer, Concerning Baptism*
(London and New York, 1919), pp. 38-39.   Tertullian
treats the question of veiling in a later work, *De Virginibus Velandis* (see edition of E. Dekkers in *Corpus
Christianorum,* Series Latina, ii, 1209-1226).

dress and to scorn the use of make-up as a means to augment natural beauty.[75] Erasmus, centuries later, was to issue similar warnings to the religious women reading his *Virginis et Martyris Comparatio*.[76]

Erasmus tells us that the Latin Christian poet Prudentius, when choosing as his theme the praise of martyrs or virgins, soared to greater heights than did Pindar and Horace.[77] It seems likely that the great Renaissance humanist had in mind certain poems of Prudentius found in the *Peristephanon Liber*.[78] In the fifth poem of this group, *Passio Sancti Vincenti Martyris*, the Machabean brothers are respectfully mentioned as martyrs;[79] and in the tenth, *Sancti Romani Martyris Contra Gentiles Dicta*, their inspiring story is recounted by a Christian woman encouraging her son to withstand torture by reminding the boy of the seven brothers and their heroic mother.[80] In the fourteenth poem, *Passio Agnetis*,

---

[75]*De Cultu Feminarum*, ed. by A. Kroymann, in *Corpus Christianorum*, Series Latina, i, 343-370.

[76]*Opera Erasmi*, v, 499 (lines 2-37); Paynell tr., pp. 57-63.

[77]*Opera Erasmi*, v, 496 (lines 49-52); Paynell tr., p. 37.

[78]This work is found in vol. ii of *Prudentius*, English trans. by H. J. Thomson, Loeb Classical Library, 2 vols. (Cambridge, Mass., and London, 1949-1953).

[79]*Prudentius*, ii, 201.

[80]*Ibid.*, ii, 276-281. This poem concerning St. Romanus may have originally been written as a separate book; see vol. i of *The Poems of Prudentius*, tr. by Sister M. Clement Eagan, C.C.V.I., in Fathers of the Church, xliii (1962), 190-191, n. 1. An account of St. Romanus is found in the work of Eusebius *De Martyribus Palaestinae*: see Migne, *Patrologia Graeca*, xx, cols. 1463-1470 (ch. II); English trans. by A. C. McGiffert in *Nicene and Post-Nicene Fathers*, i, 343-344 (ch. II).

Prudentius describes the brave death of St. Agnes, who is reverently referred to by Erasmus, and concludes with an encomium of this virgin martyr of the early Church.[81]

Perhaps with the exception of the Scriptures themselves, no works seem to find a stronger echo in *Virginis et Martyris Comparatio* than do those of St. Jerome. In one of his most celebrated letters, that addressed to the virgin St. Eustochium,[82] this great Latin Father has included numerous citations and examples which were later to be found in the work of Erasmus written for the nuns of Cologne. For instance, St. Jerome quotes frequently from the *Canticum Canticorum* certain passages to be included in Erasmus's treatise.[83] He refers to the parable of the wise and foolish virgins[84] and repeats approvingly the praise of virginity in the Apocalypse.[85] There are, of course, the references to Christ's counsel of religious celibacy,[86] as well as to St. Paul's words on the same subject.[87] A quotation from the same Apostle, used also in the work of Erasmus, is in-

---

[81]*Prudentius* (Loeb Classical Library), ii, 338-345.

[82]Epistola XXII, in Migne, *Patrologia Latina*, xxii (1854), cols. 394-425. Erasmus mentions Eustochium, among others, as a virgin saint: *Opera Erasmi*, v, 500 (line 23); Paynell tr., p. 71.

[83]Cant. I, 3; Cant. II, 1, 10-11; in Migne, *Patrologia Latina*, xxii, cols. 399, 406, 425 (cited incorrectly in this column as Cant. I, 10-11).

[84]". . . virgines stultae, quae oleum non habentes, excluduntur a sponso": *Patrologia Latina*, xxii, col. 397. The reference is to Matt. XXV, 1-13.

[85]Apoc. XIV, 4; in *Patrologia Latina*, xxii, col. 425.

[86]Matt. XIX, 11-12; in *Patrologia Latina*, xxii, col. 406.

[87]1 Cor. VII, 7-8, 25; in *Patrologia Latina*, xxii, col. 407.

cluded in order to remind the reader that her
thoughts should be set on the rewards of
heaven.[88]

In this same epistle, St. Jerome cites examples
later mentioned in the treatise of Erasmus. The
prudent virgin, he says, should consider the lives
of Eve[89] and Dina,[90] and should rather pattern her
conduct upon that of the Virgin Mary, who con-
versed not with men but with an angel.[91] The virgin should avoid worldly company, especially the
snares of corrupt men,[92] remembering her duty of
fidelity to a religious calling.[93] St. Jerome refers
to the writings of Tertullian and St. Cyprian, and
alludes admiringly to those of St. Ambrose, very
possibly having in mind the latter's *De Virginibus
ad Marcellinam Sororem Suam*.[94] Thus it seems
reasonable to conclude that in the epistle to Eustochium, alone, Erasmus could have found sources
suggestive of many thoughts expressed in his own
treatise.[95]

However, also in a longer work of St. Jerome,
Adversus Jovinianum, one can discover ideas,
quotations, and examples which later make their
way into *Virginis et Martyris Comparatio.* In

---

[88]Phil. I, 23; in *Patrologia Latina*, xxii, col. 404 (cited
incorrectly as Phil. II, 23).

[89]Gen. III, IV, 1; in *Patrologia Latina*, xxii, col. 406.

[90]Gen. XXXIV; in *Patrologia Latina*, xxii, col. 411.

[91]Luke I, 26-38; in *Patrologia Latina*, xxii, col. 422.

[92]*Patrologia Latina*, xxii, cols. 413-414.

[93]2 Cor. XI, 2; in *Patrologia Latina*, xxii, col. 415
(no. 29).

[94]*Patrologia Latina*, xxii, col. 409.

[95]In alluding to the Essenes, St. Jerome makes a
casual reference to the description of them by Josephus
(the "Graecus Livius"), whom he compares to the Roman
historian Livy; see *Patrologia Latina*, xxii, col. 421.

writing against Jovinian, the Latin Father discusses at some length St. Paul's teaching concerning marriage and celibacy, quoting from the first Epistle to the Corinthians[96] and from the Gospel of St. Matthew.[97] Furthermore, he draws the sharp distinction between the virgin who is not spiritually motivated and the one whose celibacy is lived with an attitude of religious dedication.[98] Quoting copiously from the *Canticum Canticorum,* he maintains that this book of the Scriptures can be interpreted as containing the mysteries of virginity,[99] "virginitatis continere sacramenta."[100] Not omitting even the ancient classical world, he cites numerous examples in order to declare that virginity was held in veneration in the traditions of the Greeks and Romans.[101]

It might be of interest to add that in still another well-known composition, the shorter *De Perpetua Virginitate B. Mariae adversus Helvidium,* St. Jerome comments upon certain ideas later incorporated into the Erasmian treatise. In controverting the views of Helvidius, the Latin Father concludes his work with a defence of religious virginity.[102] In so doing, he quotes from St.

---

[96] 1 Cor. VII; see Migne, *Patrologia Latina,* xxiii (1883), cols. 228-243.

[97] Matt. XIX, 10-12; in *Patrologia Latina,* xxiii, col. 238.

[98] *Patrologia Latina,* xxiii, cols. 241-242.

[99] *Ibid.,* xxiii, cols. 263-266 (nos. 30-31). Among these quotations are Cant. I, 11, and Cant. II, 10-12, 14, 16, all of which are used by Erasmus.

[100] *Patrologia Latina,* xxiii, col. 263.

[101] *Ibid.,* xxiii, cols. 282-286 (nos. 41-42).

[102] *Patrologia Latina,* xxiii, cols. 213-216 (nos. 20-21). An English translation, by John N. Hritzu, is found in *Saint Jerome: Dogmatic and Polemical Works,* Fathers of the Church, liii, 39-43.

Paul's first Epistle to the Corinthians and refers
to the appropriate passage in the Apocalypse,[103]
he discusses some of the difficulties encountered
in marriage, and he regrets that some unworthy
persons, by their bad example, bring dishonor to
the celibate state.

It would seem quite likely that Erasmus drew
inspiration also from sources other than those so
briefly discussed in the previous few pages.[104]
Nevertheless, one can confidently assert, after
this cursory examination of certain works of
the Fathers and other early religious authors
and, above all, after a careful reading of the
Erasmian text itself, that *Virginis et Martyris
Comparatio* has its roots deep in the Scriptures
and the writings of the early Church and can
thus, as Erasmus hoped, bring forth the fruits
of piety and devotion.

THE ENGLISH EDITION

Virginis et Martyris Comparatio was translated into English by Thomas Paynell and was

---

[103]Apoc. XIV, 4. This is quoted by Erasmus: *Opera
Erasmi*, v, 494, lines 29-32; Paynell tr., p. 16. The passage is incorrectly cited in *Patrologia Latina*, xxiii, col.
215.

[104]Although in *Virginis et Martyris Comparatio*
Erasmus does not mention St. Athanasius, he was later
to publish translations of some *Lucubrationes* written
by or attributed to this Greek Father, one of which is
entitled *De Virginitate*. These works appeared as additions to some translations Erasmus made from St.
John Chrysostom (pub. Basel, 1527). See Allen, vi,
467-470 (ep. 1790 and commentary), 483 (commentary
on ep. 1800). St. Athanasius's authorship of *De Virginitate* is doubtful; see V. C. De Clerq in *New Catholic
Encyclopedia s. v.* "Athanasius, St.," i, 998. The treatise
is found in Migne, *Patrologia Graeca*, xxviii (1887), cols.
251-282. Also, it may be noted, that Erasmus quotes

published by Thomas Berthelet, London, 1537, as *The Comparation of a Vyrgin and a Martyr*. The English volume includes, in addition to the text itself, a dedicatory preface placed between the title-page and the text. This preface is addressed by the translator to "John Ramsay, lorde priour of Merton," a prominent monastic establishment in the England of the early Tudors. There is no translation of Erasmus's dedicatory epistle to Helias Marcaeus.[105]

The signatures of the English edition are numbered in octavo, the translated text extending from A.ii. as far as, and including, [E.vii.], on the verso side of which is the colophon. In addition to the signatures, which appear at the bottom, the recto sides of all the leaves are designated at the top by Arabic numerals, the translated text beginning at 2 and ending at 39. Unfortunately, there are errors in the foliation, in both the signatures and the Arabic numerals.[106]

An extant copy of Paynell's translation, *The Comparation of a Vyrgin and a Martyr,* can be found in the Lambeth Palace Library in London.[107] It is this copy which is reproduced in fac-

---

from a pre-Christian Latin poet: Ovid, *Heroides*, "Sappho Phaoni," lines 77-78 (Paynell tr., p. 59).

[105]See footnote 15.

[106]Folios 20, 30, and 36 are incorrectly designated as 02, 03, and 39 respectively (folio 39 is given its correct designation). The numeral 4 of folio 34 is incorrectly printed. There is no signature for A.v.

[107]The work is not listed in *A Short-Title Catalogue of English Books 1475-1640* (London, 1946), but is mentioned in *A Finding-List of English Books to 1640 in Libraries in the British Isles*, compiled by David Ramage *et al.* (Durham: Council of Durham Colleges, 1958), p. 96. See also S. R. Maitland, *List of Some of*

simile in this volume by courtesy of The Most
Reverend and Right Honorable Arthur Michael
Ramsey, Archbishop of Canterbury.

Thomas Paynell, as well as John Ramsey, was
a member of Merton Priory, Surrey, a foundation
of the order of Augustinian Canons Regular. This
particular religious community could trace its
history back to the years of Henry I.[108] Since
Merton was one of the larger houses of the Aus-
tin canons in England,[109] it is not surprising to
find it as a patron of St. Mary's College, Oxford,
an establishment which served students from
various abbeys and priories of the order.[110] Nor
should it seem strange that Erasmus, himself an
Augustinian canon, made St. Mary's his Oxford
residence in the autumn of 1499, the year of his
first sojourn in England.[111]

---

the Early Printed Books in the Archiepiscopal Library
at Lambeth (London, 1843), pp. 199-200 (no. 439); William Thomas Lowndes, The Bibliographer's Manual of
English Literature, edition rev. by H. G. Bohn (London,
1857-1864), ii, 750; W. Carew Hazlitt, Bibliographical
Collections and Notes on Early English Literature, 2nd
Series (London, 1882), p. 205.

[108]According to a quaint tradition, a stone building
was thus constructed: "the founder himself laying the
first stone with great solemnity, the prior the second,
and the brethren, then thirty-six in number, each one."
The founder referred to was probably Gilbert Norman.
See Sir William Dugdale, Monasticon Anglicanum, ed.
by Caley, Ellis, and Bandinel (London, 1817-1830), vol.
vi, pt. I, p. 245; also p. 247, for "Cartae ad Prioratum
de Merton, in Comitatu Surregiae, spectantes."

[109]Dom David Knowles, The Religious Orders in England, vol. ii: The End of the Middle Ages (Cambridge,
1955), p. 259.

[110]Ibid., ii, 28.

[111]Emerton, pp. 64-65; Preserved Smith, Erasmus:
A Study of His Life, Ideals and Place in History (London and New York, 1923), p. 63.

John Ramsey, who had received from Oxford both a degree in Arts and later, in 1522, a baccalaureate in Divinity, afterwards became prior of St. Mary's.[112] A still further honor was bestowed upon him when, in the January of 1530, the canons of Merton elected him their prior.[113] It would seem that he still held this latter office by approximately the year 1537, the date of publication by Berthelet of "The Comparation," for in the dedicatory preface Paynell addresses him as prior and states further that he made the translation at Ramsey's request.

Merton Priory surrendered to the crown in the April of 1538,[114] and Ramsey soon afterwards may have begun to feel attracted to changing principles in religious thought, as the nature of two of his writings would seem to indicate: (1) A corosyfe to be layed hard vnto the hartes of all faythfull professours of Christes gospel (1548?);[115] (2) A plaister for a galled horse, 1548.[116] Ramsey died in 1551, having been dur-

---

[112]Anthony à Wood, *Athenae Oxonienses* (London, 1691-1692), i, 653, 666 (both under "Fasti Oxonienses"); W. A. Shaw in *Dictionary of National Biography s.v.* "Ramsay, John," xvi (1909), 700.

[113]Shaw in *D.N.B.*, xvi, 700; Alfred Heales, *Records of Merton Priory in the County of Surrey* (London, 1898), p. 331.

[114]A. F. Pollard in *D.N.B. s.v. "Paynell, Thomas,"* xv (1909), 572.

[115]*S.T.C.* 20661; Lowndes, iv, 2043; Shaw, in *D.N.B.*, xvi, 700, describes it as "protestant and evangelical in tone."

[116]The *S.T.C.* entry 20662 adds this phrase in square brackets: "A protestant pamphlet in verse." Lowndes, iv, 2043, and Shaw, in *D.N.B.*, xvi, 700, both describe this work of Ramsey as anti-Catholic in tone.

ing approximately his last six years or more the
rector of Woodchurch in Kent.[117]

To reconstruct the life of Thomas Paynell, the
translator, would be a task not without difficulties.[118] It seems possible that he received part
of his earlier education at St. Mary's,[119] and it is
not unlikely that in 1520 he was studying at
Louvain.[120] By the January of 1530 he had probably been already a canon of Merton Priory for a
few years, because at this date he was an acolyte
and took part in the election of John Ramsey as
prior.[121] It was almost certainly during the following years that Paynell, at Ramsey's request,
made his translation of *Virginis et Martyris Comparatio* and prepared it for the eventual publication in 1537. In 1538, at the time of the dissolu-
tion of the priory, Paynell was still a canon at

---

[117]Shaw, *D.N.B.*, xvi, 700.

[118]The article by A. F. Pollard in the *D.N.B.*, xv, 572-
574, should not be read without consulting also the fol-
lowing accounts, which afford necessary clarification or
additional information. These are three letters in the
London *Times Literary Supplement*, vol. xxx (1931):
H. Salter, p. 116 (Feb. 12); A. F. Pollard, p. 154 (Feb.
26); H. Salter, p. 199 (Mar. 12). Also consult W. H.
Stevenson and H. Salter, *The Early History of St.
John's College Oxford* (Oxford, 1939), pp. 133-136;
Heales, pp. 331, 348-349.

[119]Wood, i, 112.

[120]In this year, Thomas Lupset directed a letter
(March 31) to a Thomas Paynell at Louvain. This
Thomas Paynell was studying theology with Wilfrid Lee,
whose brother Edward (later Archbishop of York) had
written against Erasmus. See John Archer Gee, *Life
and Works of Thomas Lupset* (New Haven, 1928), pp.
75, 78, 303-304.

[121]Heales, p. 331.

Merton, for his name appears on the document of surrender.[122]

During the stormy period of religious changes that included the latter years of the reign of Henry VIII, the reigns of Edward VI and Mary, and the early years of the reign of Elizabeth I, Paynell seems to have remained unmolested. Up to the time of his death, probably in 1564,[123] he apparently held various ecclesiastical positions and also was able to devote much of his time to literary pursuits.

Paynell's known writings number more than twenty, about three fourths of them being translations. The others consist of compilations, a preface for a book on measuring land, and a subject index for William Rastell's great 1557 folio edition of St. Thomas More's English works.[124] Concerning the translations, the Erasmian scholar will find interest in the knowledge that

---

[122]*Ibid.*, pp. 347-349, cxvii (app. CLI). A photograph of the signatures affixed to the document, including those of Ramsey and Paynell, faces p. 348.

[123]The will of a "Thomas Paynell, preste" was proved March 22, 1563/64; see vol. II of *North Country Wills*, vol. cxxi of the pub. of the Surtees Society (Durham and London, 1912), pp. 24-25. Also, the fact that a few translations made by Paynell were published during the early years of Elizabeth's reign supports the probability of his living on until the year 1564.

[124]A list of Paynell's known works can be found on pp. xvii-xviii of the introduction to the facsimile edition of *The Complaint of Peace* (New York: Scholars' Facsimiles & Reprints, 1946), a translation made by Paynell of the *Querela Pacis* of Erasmus and published in 1559. This list may be subject to revision or additions because of the scarcity of information as yet available concerning Paynell. With like caution the reader might also peruse the account of Paynell's life, on pp. xiii-xvii, preceding the list of writings.

Paynell was the first to render into English two
works of the great Dutch humanist, *De Contemptu Mundi*[125] and the *Querela Pacis*,[126] and that the
first English translation of *Virginis et Martyris
Comparatio* was probably Paynell's "The Comparation of a Vyrgin and a Martyr."[127] Paynell
also translated Erasmus's *De Civilitate Morum
Puerilium Libellus,* but this edition was published
in 1560,[128] many years after the publication of
Robert Whittington's translation of the same
work.[129]

One who views Paynell's work as a whole—
translations, compilations, dedicatory prefaces—
must needs be favorably impressed by the translator's service to literature. This contribution,
beginning with what was probably his first publication, in 1528,[130] lasted during a period of more
than thirty years. Not only was this period one
of change and, at times, even turbulence for him
and his countrymen, but Paynell was further committed first to the obligations of monastic life
and, later, to the pressures of ecclesiastical du-

[125]*S.T.C.* 10471.

[126]*S.T.C.* 10466.

[127]The *S.T.C.* makes no reference under Erasmus to
this work. But it is noted as a first English edition by
Willian H. Woodward in his list of "First Editions of
Erasmus in English, XVI. Century," in *Desiderius Erasmus concerning the Aim and Method of Education* (Cambridge, 1904), p. 239.

[128]Paynell's translation, *The Civilitie of Childehode,*
was probably from a French version; see W. Carew
Hazlitt, *Handbook to the Popular, Poetical, and Dra-
matic Literature of Great Britain* (London, 1867), p.
101.

[129]Whittington's translation is dated 1532; see
S.T.C. 10467.

[130]*S.T.C.* 21596.

ties. Yet he was able throughout these years to give to contemporary readers translations not only of Erasmus but also, among others, of St. Cyprian,[131] Agapetus,[132] Vives,[133] Ulrich von Hutten,[134] and Cuthbert Tunstall.[135] To do this was no mean achievement.

THE TRANSLATION OF PAYNELL

No study of *The Comparation of a Vyrgin and a Martyr* would be complete without a short commentary indicating certain features of Paynell's method of translating.

(1) What is immediately obvious is that the translation abounds in doublets; if one considers style only, this usage frequently appears unnecessary and commonplace. A few examples will suffice: *munuscula*, "giftes and presentes";[136] *factis*, "actes and dedes";[137] *ornatur*, "ornated and decked";[138] and *sentire*, "haue or fele."[139]

There are, however, instances where Paynell's use of doublets seems to add significance to the Latin word and occasionally give an almost poetic quality to the original: for example, *labefactari* becomes "fall in ruyn nor decay";[140] *felicius*,

[131]*S.T.C.* 6156.
[132]*S.T.C.* 193.
[133]*S.T.C.* 24855.
[134]*S.T.C.* 14024.
[135]*S.T.C.* 24318.
[136]*Opera Erasmi*, v, 493 (line 11 of text); Paynell tr., p. 4.
[137]*Opera Erasmi*, v, 493 (line 17 of text); Paynell tr., p. 5.
[138]*Opera Erasmi*, v, 499 (line 22); Paynell tr., p. 61.
[139]*Opera Erasmi*, v, 500 (line 27); Paynell tr., p. 72.
[140]*Opera Erasmi*, v, 493 (line 27 of text); Paynell tr., p. 7.

"more plesante and more welthy" ;[141] and *dissimu-
lata,* "cloking and hydynge."[142]

(2) The translator often employs doublets to
produce vivid alliteration. He effects this by
translating one word: *sordidata* to "slubbred &
soylled,"[143] or by rendering a phrase: *terrore mor-
tis* to "the verye terrour and drede of dethe."[144]
He can use alliteration by expanding on one
word: the adjective *immarcescibilem* to "euer-
more freshe and flourysshynge,"[145] and the noun
blandimentis to "fals flatering vanities."[146] The
reflexive *se colit* becomes "make her selfe gorgious and gay."[147]

(3) The translator shows an ability to avoid
excessive dependence on Latinisms. Although
one finds "captation" for *captatio*[148] *and* "magnifycent" for *magnifica,*[149] nevertheless, on the whole,
Paynell is adept in using English idiom. He
renders *Nutu* by the prepositional phrase "with
tournynge of an hande,"[150] and *angustus* becomes
"strayt and narowe."[151] He amplifies *felicem co-
piam* by giving us "aboundaunt and flowynge

---

[141]*Opera Erasmi,* v, 499 (line 48) ; Paynell tr., p. 65.
[142]*Opera Erasmi,* v, 500 (line 16) ; Paynell tr., p. 70.
[143]*Opera Erasmi,* v, 499 (line 27) ; Paynell tr., p. 61.
[144]*Opera Erasmi,* v, 498 (lines 10-11) ; Paynell tr.,
p. 49.
[145]*Opera Erasmi,* v, 495 (line 5) ; Paynell tr., p. 20.
[146]*Opera Erasmi,* v, 498 (line 30) ; Paynell tr., p. 53.
[147]*Opera Erasmi,* v, 499 (line 8) ; Paynell tr., p. 58.
[148]*Opera Erasmi,* v, 493 (line 8 of text) ; Paynell tr.,
p. 4.
[149]*Opera Erasmi,* v, 500 (line 44) ; Paynell tr., p. 76.
[150]*Opera Erasmi,* v, 493 (line 18 of text) ; Paynell tr.,
p. 5.
[151]*Opera Erasmi,* v, 500 (line 35) ; Paynell tr., p. 74.

style,"[152] and the infinitive *peregrinari* becomes a picturesque clause: "she trauayleth as a pilgrim farre."[153] He wisely refrains from attempting to imitate the reverent play on words Erasmus employs in describing the spiritual joy of consecrated virgins:

. . . sibique gratulantes, quod
pure puro puros hymnos modulantur.

. . . and to them selfe demeanyng great gladnes, that they being pure and chaste, do singe pure and cleane balades in honour of their pure and clene spowse.[154]

(4) Paynell shows also a freedom from excessive dependence on Latin construction. This can be observed from simple examples. The phrase *ante proditum Evangelium* becomes a clause: "before the gospell was shewed or knowen to the worlde."[155] Also, the adjective *exoptabile* (with a negative) is changed to a clause: "you shulde not desyre it."[156] The ablative absolute *patris arce relicta* is rendered "lefte his fathers most royall palaice."[157] The translator is capable of amplifying a thought expressed originally in terse, compact style:

---

[152]*Opera Erasmi*, v, 496 (line 52) ; Paynell tr., p. 37.
[153]*Opera Erasmi*, v, 498 (line 41) ; Paynell tr., p. 55.
[154]*Opera Erasmi*, v, 494 (line 34) ; Paynell tr., pp. 16-17.
[155]*Opera Erasmi*, v, 497 (line 41) ; Paynell tr., p. 45.
[156]*Opera Erasmi*, v, 500 (line 20) ; Paynell tr., p. 71.
[157]*Opera Erasmi*, v, 500 (line 16) ; Paynell tr., p. 70.

Martyr tradit corpus suum, uirgo subigit
& in spiritus seruitutem redigit.

A martyr deliuereth his body to be persecuted: A virgin kepethe her body in
lowe subiection, and maketh it obedient
vnto the spirite.[158]

But in a sentence praising the heroic mother of
the seven Machabean martyrs, Paynell demonstrates equal skill in using emphasis that is un-
adorned and best suited to the idiom and rhythm
of English prose:

Virginitatis exemplum ex se praebere
non potuit, sed quod potuit, magno stu-
dio praestitit.

Of her self she coude gyue none example
of virginitie, but she perfourmed and
dyd as moch as laye in her to do.[159]

(5) In conclusion, one might raise the question, whether in *The Comparation of a Vyrgin
and a Martyr* Paynell composes any passages
which have the majestic glow of some which appear in his other translations. The reader recalls with truly aesthetic delight the description
of the monastic landscape in *De Contemptu
Mundi*,[160] and he remembers the haunting beauty

---

[158]*Opera Erasmi*, v, 498 (lines 35-36); Paynell tr., p.
54.

[159]*Opera Erasmi*, v, 497 (lines 29-30); Paynell tr., p.
41.

[160]Paynell's translation of *De Contemptu Mundi* of
Erasmus (Gainesville, Florida: Scholars' Facsimiles &
Reprints, 1967), pp. xxvi-xxvii of the Introduction, and
pp. 80-81 of the facsimile text.

of the mournful yet consoling prayer of Cuthbert
Tunstall "for the dede which haue no man that
praieth for them."[161]

The answer to the question may be that one
will not find in *The Comparation* any gems of such
striking brilliance as those just cited from other
renderings. This does not, however, in any way
imply that the prose of *The Comparation* is not
of the highest quality. To grasp the excellence
of Paynell's style in this work, the reader need
refer only to a few passages such as the following,
found near the beginning of the treatise:

> . . . I perceyue ye seke for spiritualle
> gayne, with your pleasaunt and swete
> gyftes, delytynge the mouthe, diligently
> labourynge to opteyne of me those
> thynges, that fede the sowle: this is a
> very deuout captation, a holy desyre, a
> ryght wyse and gaynfull chaunge, and
> mooste comely and seemely for wyse
> virgins: yf I were the man that coude
> bring forthe any thynge oute of the se-
> crete coffers of holy Scripture, that
> might in like maner refreshe your
> myndes, as your giftes and presentes do
> refresshe my bodye. You erre not in
> youre affeccyon, but you faylle in youre
> election: you loue that that is beste, but
> you chose not him, that can satisfie your
> holy desyres. And yet bicause you shal
> not thynke me vtterly vnkynde, I do

---

[161] Paynell's translation of this prayer is given in
Charles Sturge, *Cuthbert Tunstal* (London, New York,
and Toronto, 1938), p. 387.

not a lyttell reioyce, to see in you
(chosen virgyns of god) this good
mynde, that is, thyrstynge nothynge els
but the glory of your spouse.[162]

The foregoing passage clearly demonstrates that
the translator has achieved mastery of a mature
English style. The reader, of course, immediately
notices the employment of the doublet and alliteration; but in the case of the latter, the use
can be at once ornate and discriminating, as in
"spiritualle gayne . . . swete gyftes," and it is not
always overt, as in the delightful phrase "the
secrete coffers of holy Scripture." There is also
frequent use of parallelism blended with antithe-
sis. And the translator, furthermore, shows a
feeling for prose rhythm whereby he can end his
thought with the emphasis characteristic of a
periodic sentence.

Should one require further examples of Paynell's mastery of stylistic devices, he might read
beyond the passage just quoted. In the nineteen
lines following,[163] the translator again employs alliteration and parallelism, and he also makes use
of chiasmus.[164] And to reassure himself that
Paynell possessed this mastery not only when
translating the work of others but also when
composing original prose, the reader might

---

[162]Paynell tr., pp. 4-5. See *Opera Erasmi*, v, 493
(lines 6-15 of text).

[163]Paynell tr., line 5 of p. 5 to line 2 of p. 6; see
Opera Erasmi, v, 493 (lines 15-19 of text).

[164]The last sentence of the nineteen lines: "He made
the worlde . . . that that he made." Paynell tr., pp. 5-6;
Opera Erasmi, v, 493 (lines 18-19). The sentence of
Erasmus is in regular parallelism.

peruse the dedicatory preface.[165] Here he will observe an English style that shows the influence of the Renaissance: subordination in sentence structure along with the rhetorical devices and figures of speech taught by the prominent English rhetoricians of Tudor days.[166]

If Paynell is not accorded a place with the more celebrated English prose masters of the early sixteenth century—with St. Thomas More, Tyndale, Elyot, and Ascham—his contribution is certainly not insignificant. By his translations he made available to the reading public of his time many books on a variety of subjects. And, equally important, his writing was part of that movement which resulted in a fine and pure English prose. He deserves to be remembered.

CONCLUSION

In the *Catalogus Lucubrationum* Erasmus had mentioned *Virginis et Martyris Comparatio* as a work which should lead the reader in the way of devotion. A few years later, in a letter to Aemilius de Aemiliis,[167] dated Freiburg-im-Breisgau, May 17, 1529, he once more refers to certain of his compositions "quae minus habent inuidiae, et plus conducunt ad pietatem," and among these

---

[165]P. 2.

[166]Ian A. Gordon, *The Movement of English Prose* (Bloomington, Indiana, and London, 1966), pp. 77-79.

[167]Aemilius translated Erasmus's *Enchiridion* into Italian (pub. 1531); see Allen, viii, 142-144 (ep. 2154 and commentary, esp. n. 14 at bottom of p. 143). Aemilius states that he rendered the work "in Ethruscam" (p. 143), but most likely he refers to the vernacular tongue then spoken in Tuscany; see Allen, vi, 475, n. 57.

works conducive to piety he again places *Comparatio Virginis et Martyris* and *De Immensa Dei Misericordia Concio.*[168]

With this judgment of Erasmus it is difficult for any reader of *The Comparation* not to agree. If other writings of the great Dutch humanist seem often satiric and at times bitter in their treatment of monasticism, their author did respect those men and women who lived the conventual life according to its ideal of imitating Christ as far as was possible.[169] The *Virginis et Martyris Comparatio* is evidence of this respect for the ideal of observing the evangelical counsels. And it is in this treatise, beyond the turmoil and controversy of the changing times, that Erasmus is willing to extol those persons who essay a total Christian commitment—*propter regnum caelorum.*

WILLIAM JAMES HIRTEN

Siena College
Loudonville, New York
August, 1969

---

[168]Allen, viii, 176 (ep. 2165).

[169]The reader is referred to remarks in certain letters written by Erasmus during approximately the last nine years of his life: to a monk (October 15, 1527), Allen vii, 200 (ep. 1887, lines 23-50); to Louis Ber (March 30, 1529), Allen, viii, 120 (ep. 2136, lines 194-202); to John of Heemstede (February 28, 1533), Allen x, 164 (ep. 2771, lines 71-101). Translations of these three passages can be found in vol. ii of John J. Mangan, *Life, Character & Influence of Desiderius Erasmus of Rotterdam* (New York, 1927), pp. 276, 312-313, and 346-347 respectively.

ACKNOWLEDGMENTS

In the preparation of an edition of this kind, it is always difficult to render sufficient thanks to those without whose assistance the enterprise could not be successfully concluded. But I confidently hope that this difficulty can be surmounted, if not by adequacy of words, at least by the sincere gratitude I feel towards those who have so kindly lent me their aid.

First and foremost, I wish to express my deep appreciation to the Most Rev. and Right Hon. Arthur Michael Ramsey, Archbishop of Canterbury, and to the trustees of the Lambeth Palace Library of London for graciously permitting me to use their library copy of *The Comparation of a Vyrgin and a Martyr* for facsimile reproduction in this volume. I wish also to express my thanks to Mr. E. G. W. Bill, the Librarian, who so kindly gave of his time in arranging for the preparation and shipment of the microfilms.

Since almost all my research was carried on in the Library of the Yale University Divinity School, I wish to record my debt of gratitude to Dr. Raymond P. Morris, the Librarian, and to Miss Helen B. Uhrich and Miss Jane E. McFarland, all of whom most kindly aided me by their friendly assistance and helpful suggestions.

Finally, I desire to acknowledge the kindness of Professor Robert Hood Bowers, who graciously consented to review the introduction, and of Dr. Harry R. Warfel, the General Editor of Scholars' Facsimiles & Reprints, who saw this edition through the press in so tireless and friendly a spirit.

W. J. H.

DESIDERIUS ERASMUS of Rotterdam
to the most upright and learned
FATHER HELIAS MARCAEUS,
director of the Machabean nuns and
of the most distinguished
Convent of the Machabees,
sends greetings.*

We are sending a little volume, both brief in extent
and late in arrival; nevertheless you may acknowledge it
as both copiously written and sufficiently expedited, if
you could understand how no leisure time is left to me
for obliging my friends in matters of this kind because
of continual infirmities, almost perpetual business, now
in other things and then principally in sending and receiving letters, and afterwards the toil involved in studies
and yet demanded by the subjects undertaken.

If your good-will has been satisfied, I ardently re-
joice; if not quite, it is proper that you at least be con-
tent with the manifest good-will of our friendly inten-
tion, if only so that your kindness be not falsely pro-
claimed to us. When more leisure time will permit, we
shall satisfy your devout wish in richer abundance.

Farewell, best of men; may you thrive, along with
your esteemed choral band of virgins rendering service
to God.**

Basel, July 30, 1524

---

*The preface to the *Virginis et Martyris Compa-
ratio*; see *Opera Erasmi*, v, 492. The above translation
is that of the editor of this facsimile edition, since the
preface was not rendered into English in the Berthelet
edition. See footnote 15.

**". . . of virgins rendering service to God": this
phrase, "Deo militantium virginum," is omitted in the
1540 Froben edition of the *Omnia Opera*, but is found
in the version of the preface given by Allen, v, 510 (ep.
1475 and note to line 10), 509 (commentary on ep. 1475).

THE
COM-
PA-
RATION OF
a Virgin and
a Mar-
tyr.

AN.M.D.XXXVII.

2

⌖ The preface.

⌖ To the ryght worſhypfull Maſter Iohn
Ramſay, lorde priour of Merton, Tho=
mas Paynell, chanon of Mer=
ton ſendeth gretynge.

His lyttell and fruitfull boke,
as you of your moſte gentylle
nature, deſyред me your obe=
dient, I haue tranſlated into
englyſſhe, I feare ſome wyll
ſay, moche more gladly than counnyngly,
and that my wyll was farre more redy thã
my wytte: but howe ſoo euer I haue done,
if it may pleaſe your lordſhyp, I holde me
well payde : for not only in this , But in all
other thinges, my deſyre is, to do that, that
may be acceptable to your good mynde: o=
ther that be lerned, & lyke not my trãſ=
lation, may ſette it forthe in eng=
lyſſhe more eloquently, and
ſo do bothe great pro=
ſyte and pleaſure
to many one.
Thus
god preſerue your lordſhyp
in good helthe.

ERASMVS ROTERO. TO
the venerable colledge of Byrgins Ma=
chabeticas at Coleyne, sendeth gre=
tynge in Christ Jesu, the sonne of
a vyrgin, and Crowne
of all Byrgyns.

OVR DEVOVT
myndes good vir
gyns doo ofte ty=
mes prouoke me,
with youre dely=
cate and swete p̄=
sentes, that I shoulde by somme
maner of wꝛitynge, not onely ce=
lebꝛate and laude your most pꝛe=
cyouse treasure, but also extolle
and cōmende vnto you, your in=
tent and purpose. In the tone ye
be ledde by a certayne relygious
desyꝛe, sekynge nothynge els but
the gloꝛye of god, the whyche in
his sayntis is very gloꝛious: In
A.ii.   the

In the tother I perceyue ye seke
foz spiritualle gayne, with your
pleasaunt and swete gyftes, delyp=
tynge the mouthe, diligently la=
bourynge to opteyne of me those
thynges, that fede the sowle: this
is a very deuout captation, a ho=
ly desyze, a ryght wyse and gayn=
full chaunge, and mooste comely
and seemely foz wyse birgins : yf
I were the man that coude bzing
fozthe any thynge oute of the se=
crete coffers of holy Scripture,
that might in like maner refreshe
your myndes, as your giftes and
pzesentes do refresshe my bodye.
You erre not in youre affeccyon,
but you faylle in youre election:
you loue that that is beste, but
you chose not him, that can satis=
fie your holy desyzes. And yet bi=
cause you shal not thynke me vt=
terly

terly vnkynde, I do not a lyttell
resoyce, to see in you (chosen vir=
gyns of god) this good mynde,
that is, thyrstynge nothynge els
but the glory of your spouse. For
it is an euident and a sure token
of a chast wyfe, to recken her husbandes glory her owne. For truly he, vnto whom you are specy=
ally spoused, is aboue al the children of men the moste goodlyest,
and in all his actes and dedes he
is the moste glorious : Though
oone wolde contemplate and beholde on euery syde the wonder=
full frame of this world, yet shall
he fynde hym more gloryouse in
the redemynge of the worlde, thã
in makynge therof. He made the
worlde, and the hole company of
aungelles with tournynge of an
hande : but with his precyouse

Gen. I.

A.iii.   bloud

bloudde he redemed that that he
made. The same wisedome, whi=
che is Christe Jesus, and whiche
also is the wonderfull werkman
of this worke, to thentēt to make
a thynge more meruayllous, by
dyuine crafte he edifted a howse
eternall, and a temple worthy for
god, that is the Churche, whiche
he as a kynge moste ryche, dydde
freshly garnishe and ornate with
all maner of spiritual ornamen=
tis. For what is golde, syluer, y=
uory, what is the smaragde, the
Topase, the beryll, or the varia=
ble shynynge of precious stones,
coparring them to the rich giftis
of the holye ghooste, whiche are
prophecy, the gyfte of tongues,
the vertue of working myracles,
and the curynge of infyrmities,
peace, puritie, charitie, and suffe=
rance

rance? This holle Edifice, made
of lyuely stones, with a wonderfull agrement couched together,
eyseth vp to heuen, Christ beinge
the very corner stone, knytteth
fast to gyther al the hole frame, ÿ
it can neither fall in ruyn nor decay. These stones are the dyuers
orders of saynctis. In this Tem
ple he resoyceth to dwell, lyke as
he saythe in an other place : My
delectacyons are to be with the
sonnes of men. He this magny-
fycent Salomon glorifieth hym
selfe in these rychesses : he is noo
where more meruaylous, noo
where more glorious, than in his
saynctis : to whom he hath vouchesafed this honoure, to make
them his own membres : and ac-
ceptynge them as his bretherne,
to make theym heires with hym

A.iiii. of

Act.4.

Pro.8,

of the heuenly kyngedome. He
dyed for al : but yet his moſt glo=
rye and pleaſure is in the bendis
of Martyrs, and in the compa=
nyes of vyrgyns. Theſe are the
moſt precious Jewels, of which
the churche of Chriſte dothe ſoo
ſtately auaunce her ſelfe of, the
whiche woteth nat wherof to glo
rye, but in the onely gyftes of her
ſpowſe. For what ſo euer thynge
is glorious in ſaynctis, the ſame
is the gyfte of Chriſte. O good
birgins, the delectations and or=
namentis of your ſpouſe, are dy=
uerſe and bariable. whã he goth
forth, he is beſet about with ſon=
drye precious bertues, and with
innumerable kyndes of flowers:
but the roſis of martyrs, and ly=
lyes of birgins, do mooſte ſpeci=
ally pleaſe and delyte hym. And
no

no meruayl, though he loue that
that he is hym selfe, ye wherof he
is the very fountayne to al other.
I am (sayth he) Flos *campi*, the flo= Cant, 2.
wer of the felde, and the lylie of
the valeyes . He is the prynce of
martyrs, for throughe hym mar=
tyrs are myghty and stronge. He
is the chiefe capitain of virgins,
for by him virgins do subdue the
flesshe, and the desyres thereof.
After that he descended downe to
the erthe, and hadde spredde a=
brode the fyre of charitie, wynter
passed away, and these freshe flo=
wers sprouted vp euery where in
our countreye. Howe scarse was
virginitie before? But after that
Christe had ones consecrate vir=
ginitie, howe many thousandes
of yong men and women sprang
vp sodaynly through out all the
worlde,

worlde, whiche wyllyngly gaue
them selfes to pure chastitie for
the kyngdom of god? After that
he, suffringe dethe on the crosse,
hadde taughte, that they were
very happye, that wolde dye for
goddis sake, howe many swar=
mes of men & women came forth,
that wyllyngely yea and gladly
suffered deathe for the glorye of
Christe? Doutlesse for this cause
it is, that your spouse glorieth in
the Cantycles, where he sayth e
thus, *Ryse vp, haaste you my svvete
loue and my fayre dooue, and come. For
novve vvynter is paste, the shoure is
goone, oure grounde is couered vvith
fresshe floures.*

¶ Howe barrayne shoulde our
erth haue ben, if he the same heuenly sonne had not kendled our
of hartis with ý hete his Charytie?
had

if he had not watred our mindes
with the showze of his grace?
But what flourisheth fayzer then
the Euangelicall veer? what is
moze plentyfulle? what is moze
louely? The rosis ruddy hewe a=
bydeth not longe, the beautie of
the lilye fadeth soone, wheron a
certayne Pagane wziteth thus:

Neyther smallage is lyuely,
Noz yet the shozte Lylie.

But those fresshe flowers, with
which the Churche is plentiful=
ly furnysshed, do neuer wyther a=
way. Foz Chziste is the immoztal
lylie, & gyueth immoztall grace
to his lylyes. He is the Rose im=
moztall, whose fresshe and fayze
colour dothe neuer fade, and the
same perpetuitie he gyueth vnto
his. He is called Flos campi, that is
the flower of the felde, bycause of
the

the Jewes. Fieldes be apte and
mete for tillage. Amonge the Je=
wes he was dyed with his owne
precious bloude, the whiche Je=
wes Moyses and other prophet=
tes dydde care and tylle, yet they
coude neuer cause them to bryng
forth suche fruites as they loked
fore. He was the lylie of the Wal=
leis amonge the thorny and vn=
tylled gentiles, to whom it is per
swaded, that he became man, and
was borne of the Virgin Marie
without spotte of synne. Surely
he was the euangelicall lilie, that
god the father so clothed, as ne=
uer Salomon was arrayed in al
his great glory. For why, neither
Salomon, nor yet none other,
was euer borne of a pure virgin,
defyled with no spotte of the fyrst
parent, who so euer couple them
selfe

selfe by feyth to this lilie, bycause
they are made one fleſhe and one
ſpirite with hym, they are pour=
ged from fylthy ſynnes, they re=
ceyue the fayꝛe white garment of
innocency, and be alſo made Ly=
lies. Foꝛ ſo in the ſame place fo= **Cant.2.**
lowynge ſaythe the ſpowſe, that
nameth hym ſelf a lilie: Lyke as
the lylie is amonge thoꝛnes, ſo is
my loue amonge the doughters.
what thyng els is the lily amõge
thoꝛnes? but a virgyne amonge
wyues.

℧ Matrymonye is an honeſte
thynge, but it is beſette aboute
with bꝛiers and thoꝛnes. Foꝛ ſu=
che as be maried, ſaythe Paule, **1.Cor.7.**
ſhall haue trybulacyons of the
fleſhe. If any man doubte, whe=
ther matrimonye haue thoꝛnes,
lette hym enquere of maried wo=
men

men, what greate grefes she en=
dureth, that hath to her husbāde
a frowarde felowe, a drunkarde,
a dycer, an aduoutrer, a waster,
what dysplesures growe of kins
folke, and what of wycked chyl=
drē, and than (if he thinke it best)
lette hym denye a virgyn to be a
lylie amonge thornes? A virgyn
being free from the cares of this
worlde, myndeth those thynges
that perteyne to our lorde, howe
she maye please hym : She that
is maried, as it were hyther and
thyther haled and plucked with
dyuers and sondry cares, setteth
her mynde on many thynges.
Surely all they that haue taken
on theym to folowe Christe, are
lylies, but specially virgyns. A=
monge them he the marueylous
spouse fedeth and taketh his de=
lyte,

lyte, whyche is not enterteyned with euery body. He is my deere derlyng and I his, which fedeth amonge the lilies, vntyll the day breake, and tyll the shadowes be gone. Suche flowers he gathereth, that he may make of them a garlande that neuer wythereth away in heuen: lyke as it is said in an nother place: My loue is goone downe into his gardeyne, vnto the swete smellinge beddes, that he may refresshe him selfe in the gardayns, and gather lilies. Trewely of those lylies speaketh the wyse man sayenge, Florisshe you flowers as doth the lilie, and gyue sweete sauour, and spredde out your bowes in grace, singe a songe of prayse, and blesse you oure lorde in his workes. The spouse beynge a vyrgyn, delpteth

Cant. 2.

Cant. 6.

Eccl. 39.

teth in virgins fonges. This is
the newe fonge, that the Syna=
goge knewe not, in the which fhe
was curfed, that brought forthe
no children. But there are in the
gofpell innumerable, that fynge
a newe fonge, whiche were rede=
med from the erthe, and called in
to the felowfhyp of aungels, by=

Apoc.14. caufe that they neyther mary nor
defyle theym felfe with women,
but folowe the lambe, whither fo
euer he gothe, and are withoute
fpotte before the throne of god.
There be many withoute fpot in
the fyghte of men, but happy are
they that appere fuche before the
throne of god: happye are they,
which to the laude of theyr newe
fpoufe, doo fynge a newe fonge,
inwardly reioyfyng, and to them
felfe demeanyng great gladnes,
                                        that

that they being pure and chaste, do singe pure and cleane balades in honour of their pure and clene spowse. And ofte tymes your quier to their spouse singeth this melodious songe:

¶O IESV the Crowne of vyr=gins, whom she thy mother con=ceyued, whiche alone a virgyne dyd beare, accept o moste mekest these our vowes.

¶O what greatte purytie is in this virgin, he the prince of vir=gins, and spowse and crowne of virgins, was cōceyued of the he=uenly spirite, and borne of a vyr=gin, the glorious beautie of vyr=gynite not broken. Of wyues the husbonde is the glory, but of vir gins Chryste is the glorye: The whiche dothe fede among lilyes, compassed aboute with crownes

B   of

of virgyns , hyghtynge and ad=
ournynge his ſpowſes with glo=
rie,and yeldynge to them rewar=
des. Your ſpowſe is a ſheparde,
which gaue his life foꝛ his ſhepe,
and is yet ſtylle carefulle foꝛ his
flocke. Foꝛ daily he ſaueth them,
dayly he calleth theym hoome a=
geyne that ſtraye abꝛode, dayely
he cureth, and dayely he feedeth
theym . He hathe alſo his delec=
tations, in whiche he taketh ple=
ſure, he hathe his neere felowes,
whome he calleth huſbandes, he
hath his playfeeres yonge may=
dens, whome he calleth wyues.
In ſpiritual thynges there is no
difference of ſeres, but they are
named and called after theyꝛ age
and merites. Chꝛiſt hath but one
ſpouſe, whiche is the churche, ſhe
hath many to accompanye her, ꝛ
euery

euery one of them mape be called
a spouse. The spouse selfe is but
one, and yet hath he somme, that
he derely loueth, to whom he cō=
mytteth his wyues, soo that they
also in maner may be called hus=
bandes. For if byshoppes mowe
rightously be called shepherdes,
sythe there is but one shepeherde
our lorde Jesus, what shall than
lette them to be called husbādes.
The wyues of this worlde, are
stately and proude of the gyftes
and dignitie of their husbandes,
they shewe and booste their gaye
garmentes and fresshe araye, for
such as haue no husbandes seme
as persones forsaken and desty=
tute. But the spowse Jesus, for
the despised ornamentes of this
worlde, doth gaily hight and ad=
ourne his spowses with dowe=
                B.ii.   ries

ries of the fowle:fo; the glo;ie of
the flefhe, whiche fo foone bany=
fheth away, he gyueth them im=
mo;tall glo;ie. Trewely to thofe
fpoufes, whiche folowynge the
example of the high fhepeherde,
and lyke balyant champyons in
defence of his flocke, doo not re=
fufe to dye, he gyueth rewardes.
what rewardes? not a garlande
of oken leaues, o; of laurell, not
an image, o; a title, o; fome other
lyke rewarde, that the wo;lde
fo; dedes wo;thily done is wont
to gyue in recompence: but a gar
lande euermo;e frefhe and flou=
ryffhynge in heuen, and a name
w;yten in the booke of lyfe, that
neuer fhall be blotted out by noo
age. This delitious and plefant
fpoufe, delyteth moft fpecially in
this company, which fo; all that,
　　　　　　　　　　loatheth

lotheth no wel diſpoſed perſon,be
he neuer ſo pooȝe.

℀ There foloweth in the foȝſaid
hymne. whyther ſoo euer thou
goeſt, virgins do folowe the,and
with laudes ſyngynge runne ſtyl
after the, and with theyȝ ſweete
ſonges make pleaſant noyſe.Cō=
cernyng the faſhion of the woȝld
it is an vncomely thinge,to ſee a
virgyn wyllyngely rounne after
her ſpowſe. But it were a fowler
ſyght,to ſee many virgins folow
one ſpouſe. In thingis touching
the ſoule,it is otherwiſe,foȝ there
is nothyng moȝe goodly, then to
ſe many many virgins, that nere
accompany one ſpouſe Jeſu. Noȝ
it is noo meruayle, if they runne
after hym, as they were woode,
foȝ loue of their ſpouſe.Foȝ he al=
lurethe theym to hym by ſecrete
      B.iii.   intyce=

Pfal. 44.

intycementes, whose louelynesse
passeth all humayne loue. He is
the feyzest among the childzen of
men, flowynge full of grace are
his lyppes, the whose vysage to
beholde angels esteme most high
felycytie. He bzeatheth with his
swete smellyng sauozs on whom
he wolle, and they on whome he

Cant. 1.

breatheth say: Drawe me after
the, and we shall renne in the o=
dour of thy swete smelling oynt=
mentes. They can not renne, ex=
cepte they be dzawen: they canne
not loue, excepte they be fyzste lo=
ued: And they that be alredy dza=
wen, desyze to be moze plentiful=
ly dzawen: they that rune, couet
to rune so fast, that they may ap=
pzoche yet moze nere to hym that
they loue. Trewely they felte and
percepued his lyppes to flowe
fulle

full of grace, the whiche sape: O Ioan 5.
lorde whither shall we goo? thou
haste the wordes of euerlastynge
lyfe. Al they that pfesse the name
of Christe, folowe theyr sheparde
Jesus: but they al onely his vn-
seperable feres, do folowe whyther so euer he well goo: they folow hym euen to the very beatin-
ges, they folowe him euen to the
very persecution.

℃Our lorde Jesus, what tyme
he was in this world, ofte tymes
ledde after hym greate and huge
multitudes of al sortis of people:
but whan he shulde go to Hieru-
salem to be slayn, fewe dyd accō-
panye hym, but yet fewer, whan
he bearynge his Crosse, went to-
warde the Mount of Caluerey.
But they which be the very felowes of the spouse, whiche be true
B.iiii.   vir-

virgins, coulde not at this poynt
be plucked frome they? spowse.
When he hynge vpon the crosse,
Peter, whiche was thoughte to
haue a wyfe, coulde no where be
founde, but the vyrgyns, Mary
the mother of Iesu and Iohñ, a=
bode faste by the crosse, the other
women stoode afarre of, and be=
helde what was doone. They fo=
low then, ye and that gladly and
wyllyngly: no? they folowe hym
not as dumme persons, but syn=
gynge balades , and makynge
swete melody.

℄ They that be mennes wyues
haue no leysure to be in the dan=
ces, they haue no leysure, no ma=
ny tymes they haue noo luste to
synge : they muste please they?
husbandes, they must chyde and
b?aule with they? maides and ser
uantes

uantes, & chastise theyr childzen. Our virgins, being free from all care and thought of this wozlde, do nothynge els, but in spiritual quiers, synge swete hymmes to theyz spouse. Foz they ascribe no-thynge to them selfe, but gyue al the glozy of theyz felicitie to him, to whom onely they owe al thyn-ges. He this louer deliteth in su-che maner songes, he wol, he wol his gyftes to be songe: he hateth the phariseis songis, J fast twise in the Saboth, J gyue the.x. of my goodes to the poze, J am not as other men be. The moze chast that a virgin is, the moze shame-faste she is. Here the voyce of a very virgin: Beholde the hand-   Luc.i.
mayde of our lozde. And he hath sene the humilitie of his hande-mayde. Jn the cantycles he cal-
B.b.   leth

leth his fpoufe a douue. He defi=
rethe to beholde her fhappe, and
coueteth to here her boyce: Come
fayth he, my douue out of the ca-
ues of the rockes, out of the ho=
les of the walle : O lette me fee
thy byfage, and here thy boyce,
for fwete is thy boyce, and fayre
is thy face. The foule hath his
face. The face is mofte fpecially
eftemed and iudged by the eies:
with the eies we fhewe & declare
our intet: alfo with the eies with
out boyce we fignifie the inward
affections of our myndes. The
eie of a byrgin is fymple, fhe en=
uyeth not, fhe lyeth not in a wayt
to difceyue, fhe fufpectethe none
yuell, fhe myndeth not yll. The
face of fuche oone delytethe the
fpoufe, which a lyttell after fayth
thus : Howe fayre arte thou my
loue,

loue, howe fayꝛe art thou? Thou
haste douues eies :

¶ Here some wyll saye, What
swetenes is in the complaynyng
and mourning voyce of a douue,
to delyte and please a man with?
The nyghtyngales voyce shulde
rather be called to this parable
and similitude. The rare and ve=
hemente loue maketh contynu=
alle complayntes, but yet plea=
sant and moste acceptable to the
spouse. Here a lamentyng douue:
I desyꝛe to be lowsed, and to be　Phil.i.
with Chꝛist. And agayne: O wꝛet　Rom.7.
ched man that I am, who shall
delyuer me from the body of this
deathe? Harken what an other
douue saythe, Wo is me, that I　Psal.119.
dwel so long in this woꝛld. And,　Psal.136.
By the waters of Babylon we
sate downe and wepte, whan we
　　　　　　　　　remem=

remembzed the Spon.

⸿These lamentable voices and
ful of sighynges, are most accep=
table in the eares of the spouse,
in such maner of songes he moch
delpteth.

⸿And bycause they sayd, O mer
cyfull lozde accepte our vowes, it
is tyme, that they nowe expzesse
and declare, what they wold op=
teyn of they spouse: Is it riches=
ses, is it honours, is it pleasures,
is it a kyngdome, is it long lyfe?
Foz those thinges care haue they
none, foz ẙ vehemēt loue of their
spouse hath vtterly bzoughte thē
to despise those thinges. what is
it than ? we pzaye the, encreace
our myndes yet moze largely, ᵻ
graunt, that we mowe vtterly be
ignozant of all cozruption. They
aknowlege howe great a tresure
vir=

vyrgynitie is, that is, A cleane
mynde in a bodye uncorrupte.
They also aknowlege, that what
so euer he hath gyuen theym, he
wol vouchsafe to encreace it, and
to heape benefyte vpon benefyte.
Noo vyrgyn is soo pure, whi=
che hath not, wherby she may yet
profite. For you shall scacely find
any virgin, whiche to thende the
body maye be vndefyled, offen=
deth not otherwhile in thought.
Nor trewe virginitie resteth not
only in the gyft of chastitie, but
all vyce of the mynde is the cor=
ruption of this virginitie. Who
soo euer swarueth from the true
feyth catholyke, his virginitie is
defiled. Of this purenesse spea=
keth Paule, writynge to the Co= **2, Cor. 11.**
rinthees: J haue maried you vn
to one man, to bring a chaste vir=
gine

, gine vnto Chrifte : But I feare,
, leſte as the ſerpente begiled Eue
, with his wylyneſſe, euen ſo your
, wyttes ſhulde be corrupted from
, the ſimplenes, which is in Chriſt
, Ieſu.

℄ A byrgin defyled with enuye,
backbityng, arrogancie, is wou=
ded with corruption : Therfoze
they pray, that theyr moſt muni=
ficent ſpouſe woll vouchefafe to
augment the gyftes that he hath
gyuen theym, and that he wolle
graunte them to be vtterly ig=
nozaunt of all woundes of cor=
ruption. why ſaye they vtterly?
That is nother in mynde noz in
body. what is to ſay of all? what
ſoo euer the humayne affection
doth moue and ſtyze vs to. This
vowe oz requeſt might ſeme vn-
reaſonable , ne were it that the
ſpouſe

spowſe is almyghty, and mooſte
faythfull of his pzompſe. He wol
not that his ſhal be only lyke vn=
to hym, but alſo he woll them to
be the ſelfe ſame. But let vs ad=
mytte, that no manne in this lyfe
can atteine to that, that the quier
of vyzgins dothe deſyze, yet the
requeſt of this moſte thankefull
quire ſhall not be made in vayn.
Foz that that they here thzoughe
fauour of their ſpowſe are mind-
fulle of, ſhall in the reſurrection
chance them fully thzough theyz
ſpouſes augmentynge.
There are degrees in the Chur=
che milytant, and ſoo there be in
the churche triumphant. I wote
not whether I haue taryed you
longer than I ſhulde haue done
in declarynge this hymne: Truly
I repent me not, ſyth it is ſaynte
Am=

Ambꝛoſes. ffoꝛ beſyde all other argumentis,the woꝛd of thꝛe ſyllables in the ende of euery dimeter, ſheweth who is the authour. wherin I ſuppoſe that man had not ſo moche pleaſure in the concent of the meter,as he delyted in the ſymbole of of the holye Trinitie. The churche the ſpouſe of Chꝛiſte hath many hymnes, but I wote nat whether there be any that ſing with moꝛe ioy and gladnes of al perſons,than they,whiche celebꝛate the ſpouſe in the victoꝛies of Martirs,oꝛ triumphes of virgins.

℧But nowe to retourne againe to thoſe two flowers, farre paſſynge all other moſt fragant, the Roſe and the Lilie. Lyke as the deathe of Chꝛiſte with his ſwete odour dꝛew many to the contẽpt

and

and despysynge of this lyfe: soo
the virginitie of Christe allured
many a one to the loue of chastitie. They that ar drawen of him,
beinge nowe theym selues made
flowers, haue drawen other.
Christe sayde to Peter: Folowe
me. Howe manye haue folowed
Peter? who denyeth, but that we
be moche bounde to the holy doc=
tours, the whiche (euery thynge
beynge in peace and reste) haue
taught vs the way of our lorde ?
But how many mo hath the fra-
graunt swetenes of the martyrs,
drawen to the professyon of the
gospell ? Yea howe many mo the
example of virgins? It is a gret
thynge, boldely and connyngely
to dispute of the gospelle : But
the greattest poynte is, gladly to
dye for the gospell. It is a great
　　　　　C　　　thynge

Ioan.

thynge,to despise and set nought
by the gloyye and ryches of this
woylde,but it is farre greatter to
moytifie and flee the flesshe with
the concupiscencis thereof. And
the churche knoweth to whome
she is bounde.The churche (next
Chyist) hath had none in moye ho
nour, than they, which wyllyng=
ly and gladly offred theyr bodies
to be cruelly turmented , foy the
gloyie of their spouse,and foy sa=
uation of the flocke, foy the whi=
che he hym selfe vouchesafed to
dye. They secondarily were had
in honour,whiche wyllyngly foy
the kyngdome of god gaue them
selfe holly to lyue chaste. what a
great ioye and gladnes was it to
all the Churche, whan a martyy
constantly suffred dethe foy Chyi=
stis sake? And howe great soyow
and

and lamentation, if any ſhꝛanke
backe. Agayne, Howe greattely
dyd the churche reioyce, if a birgin, that myght haue bē maried
to a man, wold rather put on the
holy baile of chaſtite, and couple
her ſelfe to her ſpowſe Chꝛyſte?
And how great ſoꝛowe was there
made, if any ſuche dydde caſte of
her bayle, and wolde be maryed
to a man? Undoubted the loſſe of
a thynge, that is moſt dere, is be=
ry greuous. with what feruente
loue dydde chꝛiſten men in tyme
paſte runne to the aſhes of Mar=
tyꝛs? Howe holy was the memo=
rie of them amonge all chꝛyſten
men, whan dayly olde men, yong
men, honeſt matrones, and bir=
gins, runne thycke and thꝛefolde
to the pꝛyſones, as it were bnto
places conſecrate to god: whan
C.ii.   they

they wold kys the cheynes, with whiche they were bounde: whan the swerde, with which they were martered, was reserued and kept amonge the holy relykes? What memorie is more ioyfull, & more hye and holy to the churche, than of Martyrs? Whan do menne synge with greatter gladnesse, than in their yerely feastis? The whose afflictions and peynes the churche calleth byctoryes, theyr turmentes triumphes, theyr deathes byrthes: nor in theyr celebratiõs is no maner mournyng, but all thynges full of ioye, fulle of gratulation, full of preysing, full of myrth and sporte. Nor the eloquence of excellent lerned mē hath ben more shewed or set forth in any argument, than in celebrating the laude and prayse of mar

tyrs

ty;s and virgins. Herein P;udē=
tius, in the kynd of verses called
Liricum carmen, exceded the greate
eloquēce of Pindarus, he passed
the elegancy of Ho;ace, not possi=
syble to be folowed. Herein the
trumpe bothe of the grekes and
latyns, soundeth out I wote not
what farre greatter and mo;e di=
uine than verse heroical. In this
argumente, Ch;ysostomus, Cy=
p;ianus, Amb;osius, Hierony=
mus, and many mo then can be
nomb;ed, excell Ciceros aboundaunt and flowynge style. what
thynge maye we coniecte to be
the cause? Truly the magnitude
of the marty;s dyd minister abū=
dāce of eloquence, the feruētnes
of they; myndes added strengthe
to they; wo;des, and deuotion a=
lacritie. Of what matter so euer
                C.iii.   they

they wꝛite, theyꝛ style is plentiful
and flowyng, But as oft as they
take in hande to endyte of martyꝛs and virgins, now as it were
by diuine inspiration, they sowne
out, I wote not what thing farre
passynge mans capacitie. Those
thynges are not doone by mans
studye, but they are bꝛoughte to
passe by inspiration of the holye
goste, the whiche woll his saynctes to be so gloꝛified, in the whiche he desyrously gothe about to
be seen most gloꝛious. We wold
graunt those thynges to be done
by man, ne were it that god (whiche inspireth the mindes of good
men) doth oꝛnate the monumen-
tes of martyꝛs and virgins with
so manifold myꝛacles. Foꝛ where
are wycked spirytes moꝛe tourmented? where are moo cured of
         gre-

greuous ſyckneſſes and diſeaſes
that no phiſitions coude heale ?
What emperour, what kynge is
he, with ſettynge vp of any ima=
ges, titles, ſteples, churches, col=
legis, commandyng diuine wor=
ſhyppes, dyd opteyne ſo greatte
honour ye in this world? Doubt=
leſſe thus god dothe honour his
martyrs, the whiche ſemed here
poore abiectes and wretched cap
tyues. Thus he honourethe his
vyrgyns, the whiche beynge as
deed to the worlde, ſette ſurely al
theyr holle hope in theyr ſpowſe
Jeſu. And they alſo aknowlege,
that what ſo euer they haue, co=
meth all of the lyberall gyfte of
theyr ſpouſe. But the glorye of
martyrs doth not lyghtly glytter
and ſhyne but after the deathe :
where as virginitie euen in this
C.iiii.   life

lyfe is ful gay and glorious. For who is so barbarous, that wyll not fauour a virgin? In the very myddes of the ruffelynge warres the fierce and cruell ennemy forbeareth virginitie. And if we beleue histories, the dumme beastis, ye the hugest, the wyldest, & most cruell of them all, beare reuerence vnto vyrgynitie. Howe greatly dydde the Romaynes in olde tyme honour the relygious virgyns, called *virgines vestales*? what a naturall worshyppe and glorie of virginitie is that, whiche ydolaters do aknowlege, whi che the barbarous ennemy dothe reuerence, which the dumme beastis doo perceyue, and to whiche the wylde beastis obeye? If soo great honour be done to the vyrgins of this worlde, howe moche more

more honorable is the virgin of
Chꝛiste? O good vyrgyne, take
on the this holy pꝛide, and repute
what so euer pleasures oꝛ honoꝛs
this woꝛld bꝛaggeth of, to be far
vnder thy dignitie. It is a holye
thyng to pꝛide in your spowse, ꝓ
a deuout thyng to gloꝛie in him,
to whome you owe all thynges.
It is also a sure thynge, trusting
faythfully in hym, to rise and re=
belle agaynst the woꝛlde, whiche
bꝛaggyngly shewethe foꝛthe his
delectable pleasures. My mynd
is not at this tyme to wꝛite, what
so euer may be sayde in the laude
and pꝛaise of martiꝛs oꝛ virgins.
You haue the bokes of Cypꝛian,
you haue the bokes of Ambꝛose,
of Tertullian and Hierome, of
which the two last, were wel nere
ouermoch in admiration of vir=
C.b.   ginitie.

ginitie. For the excellency of vir=
ginitie wolde not foo be extolled,
that the prayfe therof fhoulde be
an iniurie to chafte matrimonie.
I recyte thofe thinges mofte no=
ble byrgins for this intente, that
you maye perceyue howe happy
and fortunate your College is,
the whofe chaunce is to poffeffe
bothe thofe thynges, whiche fhe
the rich fpoufe of Chrift the chur=
che holdeth mofte fpeciall in this
worlde. For you haue in kepyng
thofe moofte fragrant and fwete
rofes, of the. vii. brethern of the
Machabees , and of theyr mo=
ther, ÿ whofe fecunditie brought
forth no children to her hufband
but to god, fhe fortunately redou
bed ÿ loffe of her virginitie, with
the martyrdome of fo many fon=
nes byrgyns. She being a virgin
brought

bȝought foȝth no frute, foȝ ẙ of al
women was giuē but to one, but
yet ſhe bȝought foȝthe bothe vir=
gins and martirs. Of her ſelf ſhe
coude gyue none example of vir=
ginitie, but ſhe perfourmed and
dyd as moch as laye in her to do.
She taughte her chyldȝen to be
virgins, ſhe exhoȝted thē to mar=
tyȝdome, and wolde haue ſuffred
martyȝdome befoȝe theym, ſaue
that ſhe feared their conſtancye,
by reaſon of their tender youthe.
And ſoo the gloȝie of vyȝginitie
chanced not to the mother alyke
with the chyldern, but touchyng
the martyȝdome, the laude of the
mother is ſoo moche the moȝe, in
that ſhe beholdynge the cruelle
turmentes, ſuffred in eche of her
lyttel chyldȝen, what ſoo euer the
cruell tourmentours coude do to
the

the bodies of them. This is moꝛe
ſtronger, then bp turmentyng at
ones to be rpdde from all peyne.
ffoꝛ the parētes are moꝛe cruelly
tourmented in the perſecutynge
of their chylderne than in theym
ſelfe. And that knowethe ryghte
well the wytty crueltie of tyꝛan=
tes, which wꝛeſte out bp turmen=
tyng of the chyldꝛen in theyꝛ pa=
rentes ſighte, that they coude by
no maner of turmentes gette of
the parentes. Howe oft ſawe ſhe
beynge a woman and a mother,
her owne fleſhe and bowels toꝛre
and rente to pieces? where was
nowe the feble freiltie of ẙ kynd?
where was the tender loue and
pitie that is wont to be moꝛe be=
hement in mothers then in men?
Surely her deuout affection to
godwarde, ouercame al humain
pitie,

pitie,and her feruent feythe ouer
came the feblenes of womanhed.
All hayle mooste happy virago,
whiche haste gyuen exaumple of
fortitude to all menne. All hayle
moste fayre lyttell floures of the
churche, whiche as rype delyca=
cyes before your tyme, you haue
preuented the springe tyde of the
gospell, and haue made a shewe
of euangelycal vertue,before the
gospell was shewed or knowen
to the worlde . For as yet this
voyce of hym, which being a vir
gin,is borne of a virgin,was not
harde, Blessed be they,that haue Mat.19.
gyuen them selfe to lyue in chastitie for the kyngedome of god,
And yet the same prayse you by
preuention haue opteyned afore
hande . Nor this was not as yet Mat.16.
harde,who so wil be my disciple, Mat.8.
let

lette hym take vp his crosse and
folowe me, but you as fore run=
ners, dydde adumbrate Christis
passion. And nowe your sowles
in heuen doo folowe the lambe,
whither so euer he goeth:But as
for your vndefiled bodies (whi=
che were partners of your tour=
mentes and peynes,so in tyme to
come you shall recepue theym to
the felowshyp of euerlastyng fe=
licitie) there was noo place more
comely nor more conueniente to
kepe them in, than in a holy col=
lege of virgins.

℩ Nowe to you good vyrgyns,
that be the kepers of this so gret
a treasure, my wordes do theym
adresse. You haue in these yonge
children both an example of cha=
stite, which you ought to folow,&
a crowne of martyrdome, that
you

you shoulde extolle , glozyfienge your spouse, which stroue in thē, whiche in them gote the victozie, whiche in them dothe triumphe. He hath in one self basket Lylies myngled with roses. The bzyght beautie of the tone strpueth with the tother,noz yet the tone is not dusked oz defaced of the tother: but ẏ tone by reason the tother is with him,doth ẏ moze gaily glit= tet and shyne,lyke as whan puo= ry(as one sayd)is myngled with purpull,oz whan a shpnyng pze= cyous stone is set in yolow gold. The strpfe is so doubtefull,whe= ther is moze glozious a martir oz a virgin, that if the matter shuld be called in contention, J dare not boldly say, whiche of theyin shoulde be pzeferred the tone be= foze the tother . Bothe the tone and

and the tother are confecrate in
Chꝛift : but yet we ar moꝛe boūde
to his croffe and paffion, than to
his birginite. He giueth to them
the honoꝛable title of bleffednes,
whiche foꝛ the kyngdome of god
gyue them felfe to lyue in chafti=
tie : but yet he requirethe the fo=
lowynge of the croffe. It femeth
a greatter thyng, that whā he re=
quireth it not, yet it maketh him
bleffed, that wyllyngly wyll per=
fourme it. And in the tyme of per
fecution it is a right gret thinge,
foꝛ the gloꝛye of god to haue the
mynde alwey pꝛompte and redy
to fuffre all kyndes of deathes.
But tymes haue like as the See
hath, his tranquillities and qui=
ete caumes. And other while one
maye lefully efcape the perfecu=
ters handes . But if one be dꝛy=
uen

uen to the laſt extremitie, the dea
the of the body is the ende of gre=
uous tourmentes, and the begin
nynge of felicitie. A virgin hath
a longe and a parpetuall ſtryfe
with her houſholde ennemie, the
whiche ſhe can neyther laufullye
ſlee, noʒ eſcape by flyghte. This
houſholde fooe is the fleſhe, the
whiche whether we woll oʒ woll
not, we muſte carie about, nowe
and then rebellynge agaynſt the
ſpirite. And that it ſhal not ſeme
eaſye to any man to ſubdue this
ennemie, we haue redde of thoſe
that were ouercome with wan=
ton entycementes of the fleſſhe,
the whiche coude not be banquy=
ſhed with the verye terrour and
dʒede of dethe.

Hytherto our collation hathe
pondered, whether of thoſe two
       D   ſhulde

shulde be moze stronger: but me
semeth that virginitie in this, is
ẏ happier,that(as J by occasyon
sayde afoze) the floure of martir=
dome, doth not freshely sprede Ᵹ
flozishe, but after deathe: where
as virginitie hathe her bzyghte
beautie, her fayze fragrancy, her
grace and dignitie in this wozld.
Uirgynytie is the flower of the
sowle and mynde, but in the vy=
sage, in the eyes, and in all the
holle state of the body, there shy=
neth a certayne angelicall pure=
nesse, and a flourysshynge clere=
nesse, not acqueynted with olde
age,here as it were myndynge Ᵹ
thynkynge to be,that all we loke
foze after this lyfe, whyche lyue
deuourely and godly in Chzyste
Jesu. The mynde holle and vn=
cozrupte sparpleth abzode in the
body

bodye her bigour and strengthe,
lyke as the mynde infecte with
bices sheweth in maner a glime-
rynge lighte, or rather maketh a
grisely shewe in the selfe shappe
of the body. For carnall pleasure
is a fowle blempshe to a mannes
owne body. why doo not the bodyes of good blessed menne waxe
olde in the resurrection? bycause
nowe the soule shall rule theym,
which woteth not what olde age
meaneth. As deathe commeth of
synne, so doth syckenes and age.
Take synne away, and age shall
seme the lesse: and if age chaunce
to come, it shal chaunce more flo-
rishinge. And therfore a birgyn
recepuethe nowe in this worlde
some parte of her felicitie, exhy-
bytynge in this mortall bodye a
certayne spece or fachion of the
       D.ii.   immor=

immoztalitie to come. The pzincis of this woylde are noo mooze careful foz theyz souldiours, than they be foz the thynge that they come of, of the which whan nede requireth, they gather yong soul dyours, the whyche thynge if it shulde fayle, howe shoulde they furnysshe an armye? And nowe foz a certayne yeres there hathe ben noo suche persecution vnder chzisten pzincis, as was vsed in tyme paste vnder Nero, Domitian, Julian, and Maxentius. But whether the Chzisten feythe be in better caase vnder these oz noo, it lyeth not in me to define, surely by them it was dzawen into a narrowe poynt. But how so euer it be, if there shulde ageyne chaunce persecution, the whyche wolde require a martyz, where is

it

it moꝛe lykely that such a cōpany
shulde be gathered, than of them
the whiche despisynge al the fals
flatering vanities of this woꝛld,
haue cōsecrate theym selfes holly
to Jesu the celestiall spouse, the
which wyllyngly haue crucified
their fleshe to gether with the vi=
cis and concupiscencis thereof,
and foꝛ the loue of theyꝛ spouse,
haue contempned and sette atte
noughte that same pleasure, foꝛ
the fauour of whiche only many
moꝛtall menne desiren euermoꝛe
here to lyue. A true virgyn doth
differre very lyttell from a mar=
tyꝛ. A martir suffreth the executi=
oner to mangle his fleshe: a vir=
gin dayly dothe with good wyll
moꝛtifie her fleshe, she beinge in
maner a turmentour of her selfe.
It is somewhat moꝛe maystry to
            D.iii.   tame

tame an ennempe taken, than to
kyl him. A martyr deliuereth his
body to be persecuted : A virgin
kepethe her body in lowe subiec=
tion, and maketh it obedient vn=
to the spirite. wherfore shall the
virgin of Christ treble and feare
the handlyng of the executioner?
Shall she require rychesses, de=
lycacies, worldly pompe, world=
ly welthe, or worldly pleasures,
whiche causen other to be verye
lothe to leaue this lyfe? All these
thinges she hath now cleane for=
saken. Shall nat she, whiche lo=
ueth nothing in this world, whi=
che is deed to the worlde, whose
lyfe is onely Christe, which day=
ly maketh her turtyls mournyn=
ges, couetynge to be nerer ioy=
ned to her dere beloued spouse, &
to be imbraced & clypped of hym,
wyll

wil ſhe not (I ſay) gladly dept out
of this wꝛetched body, in the whi
che ſhe woteth wel ſhe trauayleth
as a pilgrim farre from her loꝛd?
what men haue ſuffred the tourmentes of martyꝛdom moꝛe mer
uailouſly and ſtrongly than bir-
gine Martyꝛs, Agnes, Cecilia,
Agatha, and other theyꝛ felowes
innumerable? And therfoꝛe whã
a birgin is delyuered to the exe=
cutioner, ſhe dothe not begynne
her martyꝛdome, but makethe
an ende of that that ſhe beganne
longe befoꝛe. If thoſe thynges
ſeeme to any manne ouer harde
hyghe and difficile, lette hym re=
membꝛe, that the pꝛofeſſyon of
a birgin is aboue the powers of
man, and egall with the dignite
of angels. But al they that weare
blacke bayles, are not birgins.

1.Timo.5.

Foz lyke as they (accozdynge to
faynte Paules doctryne) whiche
are true wydowes in dede, be di=
fcerned frome thofe, whiche by a
wzonge name are called wydo=
wes:and as that widowe, whych
lyueth in delytes of this wozlde,
is fayde to be deade : ryght foo a
virgin, whiche loueth any other
thynge in this wozlde thanne her
fpoufe,is not a virgin. There ar

Mat. 25 .

in the gofpel wyfe vyzgins, whi=
che by manifolde wozkes of mer=
cyand pitie, haue fo pzouided foz
them felfe, that oyle in theyz lã=
pes fhall not fayle: there are in
like maner folyffhe virgins. And

Yrcñ.1.

Pieremie bewapleth fuch vnwife
virgins : foz the dignitie of this
name is nothing mete and agre=
able foz her, the which although
her body hath not ben touched of
man,

man, yet her mynde hath ben de=
filed and spotted with filthy and
vncleane thoughtes. She that
lyueth syngle agaynste her wyll,
is maried: and she that wolde be
corrupted, if she might lefully, is
alredy corrupted. It is a thinge
of greattest difficultie, to repzesse
and kepe downe all cogitations
and inwarde thynkynges of a
wauering mynd: and yet ageinst
them assaylynge, there muste be
defence made with pzayers, re=
dynge of holy bokes, fastynges,
deueute and godly occupations:
foz why to assent to them is very
poyson. Eua the fyzste virgin,
dyd commune and talke with the
serpente, and therof spzange all
yuels: her eies were not chast, the
which the wanton intycement of
the flatterynge apple dyd adulte=

　　　　　D.b.　　　　rate

rate and defyle. The gaye costly
apparaylle, the peynted face, the
pleafant and mery enditynges of
yonge men, the propre knackes
and gyftes fente to and fro, are
playne tokens and fygnes that
virginitie dieth. For whofe plea=
fure doth a virgin ones dedicate
to Chrift, ornate and trimme her
felfe? why dothe fhe coueyte the
companye of yonge men, the whi
che toke on her the veyle of rely=
gion bycaufe the worlde fhoulde
not fe and beholde that that was
confecrate to the fpoufe Chrifte.
A woman that is maried, dothe
decke & trymme her felfe to plefe
her hufbädes eies: but why fhuld
a virgin that is maried to Chrift
make her felfe gorgious and gay
for any erthely mans pleafure?
Harke what fhe fhuld fay by the
mouthe

mouthe of a lerned poete, but a
pagane,

For whom shuld I make me fayꝛe ꝗ gay,
Oꝛ whom to pleaſe, do my diligence
whan of hym, that of my freſſe array
The oneſy cauſe is, I haue the abſence.

If she so did neglect to make her
fresh, bicauſe her huſbād was ab
ſent: how dare a virgin make her
ſelf friſke ꝗ galiard i this woꝛld,
the whoſe ſpouſe is in heuen? To
what intent doth she that is ones
betrouthed to Chꝛiſte, ſtande lo=
kynge in a glaſſe? Yea she shuld
contemplate and behold her ſelfe
in the clere fountayn of holy ſcri=
pture. Why dothe she arraye hir
ſelf in thoſe garmētes, with whi=
che he is offended? This clenly=
neſſe in the eies of your ſpowſe
ar very dirty ſpottis, this bꝛight
beautie but ſluttyſſhe beggerye,
theſe ſwete ſauours but ſtinking
ſmelles.

fmelles.He loueth a pure fpirite,
a clene foule, and a well peynted
mynde. What fo euer the worlde
hath,it is theirs,that make them
felfe gorgeous and gaye for the
worlde: the birgin of Chrifte is
more richely arrayed with defpi=
fynge of thofe thynges, thanne
with the aboundance of theym.
She is more comely apparayled
with her heares clypped of, & her
holy beyle, than any bride trym=
med in fylkes,gold,precious fto=
nes, and purpull.For the diffem=
bled beautie, fet out with feyned
colours,hath euer ben difalowed
of the Gentyles. The fpowfe of
Chrifte hath as many frefhe gar=
mentes,that make her gay in the
fyght of god, as fhe for her fpou=
fes fake defpyfed ornamentes of
this worlde, for precious ftones
                                    fhe

ſhe is oꝛnated and decked with vertues, in ſtede of pourpull ſhe hath charitie, foꝛ gold, wyſdome, foꝛ fepned colours ſymplenes of mynde, foꝛ ſylkes chaſtitie and ſhamefaſtenes: foꝛ bꝛoches and iewels, ſobꝛenes and temperance in al her woꝛdes and dedes. The fayꝛe beautie of chaſtitie can not be defyled with ſluttyſſhe gar=mentes.

It dothe appere by olde mo=numentes and wꝛytynges, howe high and ho we laudable a pꝛeiſe it was foꝛ virgins, to waſſhe the feete of myſerable creatures, to waſhe pooꝛe folkes clothes, to at tende vpon ſycke folke and ſerue thepm lowely, and foꝛ the loue of Chꝛiſt to handel and touch theyꝛ bodyes ful of ſoꝛes and botches. A virgin ſlubbꝛed & ſoylled with thoſe

those thynges, is most fayꝛe and
beautyfull in the syght of Chꝛist.
But foꝛ so moche as the institu=
tion of holy and deuout virgins,
is now otherwise, let them stryue
amonge theym selfes in the offy=
ces and woꝛkes of charitie, and
pꝛepare with theyꝛ handes, wher
with they may helpe and succour
the poꝛe andnedy. And if it hap=
pē a virgin at some tyme to haue
cōmunication with secular per=
sons, let this be her studye, that
they maye go awaye from her a=
mended by her talkynge, and she
her selfe nothynge appayꝛed. Let
the example of the fyꝛste virgine
make you moꝛe wary and sly, the
which beinge coꝛrupted by spea=
kynge with the serpente, thꝛewe
her selfe into lamentable mysery.
A yonge manne with his slypper
coun=

countenaunce, with his wanton
eies, and with his rebaud tonge,
is wo2s thã any serpent. Se that
you folowe the newe virgin, lea-
der and p2incesse of your institu-
tion, she talketh not with the serpent, but being close shutte within her secrete chaumb2es, talketh
with the angelle, and therof began all our helthe. A virgin that
talketh with an vnchaste yonge
man, speaketh with a serpente. A
virgin whiche with deuoute vowes and prayers callethe vppon
god, which hath her meditation
in holy bokes, speaketh with the
angell, o2 rather with her spouse.
Whether of these two is mooste
sure? whether is moo2e honeste?
whether is mo2e magnificent?
wherfo2e if at any tyme the desire of those thynges, the whiche
　　　　　　　　　　　as

as right swete & noble the worlo
braggyngely bosteth, shall tikyl
your myndes : cal to remembrāce
as the trouthe is, that you haue
not forgone those thiges, but to
your great lucre to haue made a
chaunge. And therfore there is
nothyng more vnfortunate than
those, which letted by carnall lu=
stis, can neyther vse the commo=
dities of this worlde, which they
mooste despre, nor yet theyr owne
pleasures. The worldly virgins
haue theyr playe felowes, they
haue theyr ornamētes, theyr spor
tes and pastymes, theyr songes
and theyr daunces, but these thin
ges such as they be, they haue no
longer than theyr freshe flouryf-
shynge and tender youthe endu=
reth. But as al these thinges are
to the virgins of Chryste trewe
and

and inwarde pleaſures, ſoo they
be euerlaſtynge. Theſe worldely
virgyns ſettynge a ſyde the garlande of virginitie, do take and
put vppon theym the mantell of
mariage, without dout (as ſaynt
Paule ſaythe) a playne token of
bondage and thraldome. But vir
gins dedicate to god, be alwaye
kepte cloſe for theyr ſpouſe, leſte
the worlde an abuoutrer ſhuld ſe
theym. For Jeſus is a ielous louer, he can not ſuffre to haue his
dere derlynges ſette and ſhewed
forthe to the ſyght of the worlde.
But whether is it more pleſante
and more welthy to be the hande
mayde of a maried manne, or the
hande mayde of Chriſte? Ecce in-
quit, *ancilla domini,* Beholde (ſayth **Luc.I.**
ſhe) the hand mayde of our lord.
Who ſo euer is truely the hande
         E   mayde

mayde of our lorde, is lady of the
world. O good virgin, interpre-
tate what thyng thy veyle betoke
neth, it is the sygne of a kyngedome, and not of bondage. They
that are veyled and couered for
theyr husbandes pleasures, doo
professe a worldly bondage. Nor
the commaundement of maryed
men, good virgins, is not alway
lyghte and easye. Often tymes
where you wende to haue hadde
husbandes, you chaunce vppon
maisters harde to please, vppon
suche as are froward and neuer
contented, vpon such as be curst
and knauishe, vpon dycers, drū-
kerdes, riotttous spenders, vpō
suche as be greatly indetted, vpō
suche as be scabbed and scuruy,
vppon frantycke felowes , and
vppon fyghters, besydes many
　　　　　　　other

other moze greuous and wycked
condicions oz diſeaſes, whiche J
ſpeake not of . Moze ouer there
foloweth care of the houſeholde,
care of childzen, buſynes of kynſ=
folke and frendes , ſtryfe in the
wozlde, lacke of childzen , bury=
enge of huſbandes. Foz why the
affliction of the fleſſhe is of noo
ſymple ſozte, the whiche ſayncte
Paule ſignifieth vnto them,that
woll rather choſe wedlocke than
virginitie. My pourpoſe is not
nowe by reaſon of this declama=
tiō to diſcriue,what ſo euer grefe
oz incommoditie foloweth mari=
age. And yet to lerne them by ex=
perience is but a wzetched wyſe=
dome : better it were to come by
the knowlege of them by redyng
the bokes of lerned men. But in
caſe you woll not gyue credence

to lerned mens wꝛitynges, than
call vnt oyou good virgyne one
of them, the whofe chaunce was
to be verye welle and welthylye
maryed, and defyre her, that fhe
woll vouchefafe to telle and de=
clare to you the true ftoꝛy of her
mariage: you fhal here fuche re=
kenynges, that you fhal nothing
repent you of your pourpofe.
Nowe lay befoꝛe your eies, the er
aumples of vyrgins, the whofe
chaunce was moofte vnluckely
and vnwelthily to be beftowed ⁊
maried, of which there is a huge
great company: and thynk thus,
that what foo euer chaunced to
them, might chance to you. what
fo euer puelles, what fo euer ca=
lamities and myferies chance to
them, that be maried to a moꝛtal
man, can in no wife hurt oꝛ greue
　　　　　　　　　　thofe,

thofe, the whiche truely, the whi=
che with harte and mynde mary
them felfe to the immoztal fpoufe
Jefu. Beleue me, your fpoufe Je
fus is in nothynge fozowfulle oz
heuy, but in al thynges pleafant
and louely. He femed fome tyme
to haue neyther fayze fhape noz
goodly beaute, but he was neuer
moze louely, than whan foz the
loue of his fpoufe he dyd vppon
hym that fame fhape and fozme.
What mayde is fhe, that wolde
not make farre moch moze of her
wower, if he being a noble mans
fonne, wolde fozfake his fathers
ryches ¢ trefure, ¢ clothed with a
homely hufbandes wiede, wolde
runne to her cotage, being a poze
mayde to the intent to opteyn her
to his wyfe? But what yf he re=
fufe not to be greuoufly woūded

in haſtynge hym to come to his
entierly beloued ſpouſe? Shuld
not he, ſo poozely clothed and all
bloudy with his woundes, ſeme
moze louely? whithout doubt he
ſhulde ſo ſeme to her that loueth
hym. Nowe thanne thynke with
your ſelfes, whether your ſpouſe
ſhulde with a ſtately countenãce
be of you diſdayned, whiche foz
your ſake lefte his fathers moſte
royall palaice, deſcended downe
into this wozld, and cloking and
hydynge the maieſtie of his dy=
uyne nature, toke vppon hym
the ſhappe and fourme of a ſer=

Phil.i.
uant, humblyng hym ſelfe to the
verye igmony and ſhame of the
croſſe. A monaſterie to a virgin
that louethe her ſpowſe, is not a
pziſon (as ſome ſklaunderouſly
do ſaye) but it is a paradyſe. It
is

is not lefull fo: you to wāder and
walke aboute whither your lufte
leadeth you : perdye this thynge
fo: virgyns is neyther furenoz
honeste, and therfoze you ſhulde
not deſpze it. Except peraduen=
ture the example of Dina plea=
ſethe you. Uirgynitie is neyther
ſozowfulle noz heuy, but a plea=
ſaunt thynge. Upzgynitie hathe
her fayze ozchardes to walke in
holye Scrypture, in the whiche
ſhe may ſpozte and play amonge
that mooſte goodlye companye
of her ſpowſe. O good lozd with
what maner companye ? With
Tecla, with Cecilia, with Aga=
tha, with Theodoza, with Eu=
ſtochio, and other innumerable.
Alſo virginitie hath her ſpiritu=
al garlādes, made and wzought
with freſſhe flowers of dyuers
                    E.iiii.   ver=

vertues: she hath her swete pom=
maunders and sauours, soo that
virgins maye say with Sayncte
Paule, *Bonus odor sumus deo in om-
ni loco*, That is to saye, We be a
good sauoure vnto god in euery
place. Also the spowse hathe his
delicate and swete spirituall po-
manders, of whiche the fragrant
swetenesse excellethe all aroma-
tike sauours. Whatte is more a=
miable than the name of Jesus?
His name is a sweete smellynge
sauour, that is sparpled abrode.
The virgins being drawen with
that sauoure, to folowe hym as
faste as they can runne, what te=
diousnesse canne they haue or fele
in this lyfe?

¶A virgin also hath her swete
pommaunder, wherwith in lyke
manet she pleaseth her spowse.

Dum

Dum esset, inquit, rex in accubitu suo, nar
dus mea dedit odorem suum, That is
to saye, when the kynge satte at
his table, he smelled my sweete
nardus. And in the gospel when
that Chꝛiste shulde be maryed to
his spowse the Churche, the wo=
man synner powred sweete smel=
lynge oyntmentes vpon hym.
Uyrgyns haue theyꝛ harpes of
Dauid, they haue the Psalter,
they haue theyꝛ songes and spi=
rytuall hymnes, with whyche in
theyꝛ hartis they synge contynu=
allye to god, gyuynge thankes,
lawdynge and besechynge, and
sommetyme with dulce and softe
syghinges despꝛinge the pꝛesence
of theyꝛ spouse, if he at any tyme
absent hym selfe foꝛ a season: foꝛ
otherwhyle he declineth and pas=
seth foꝛth by, not to the intent he

E.b. woll

woll leaue them, but to redinte=
grate and renewe his loue with
theym. what thynge haue these
worldely virgins, be they neuer
so fortunate, that may be compa=
red to these solaces and plesures?
The place canne not seme strayt
and narowe to theym, to whom
within a shorte space after the vn
measurablenes of heuen is ope=
ned: nor they canne not thynke
theym selfe to be sklenderlye ac=
compained, to whom within a ly=
tel whyle shal chance, to be in the
fel owshyppe and company of all
saynctes. why shulde I not say
within a lyttell whyle? For howe
longe I pray you, is all the holle
tyme of this present lyfe? in case
it happen a man to lyue tyl he be
very olde: whiche thynge to how
many dothe it chaunce? wher=
foze

foze good virgynes, aknowlege
your felicitie and welth, and loke
that you haue no ſpite noz enuye,
that the wozld hath his iugglyn=
ges of vayne delytes and pleſu=
res, aknowlege your dignite, and
looke not you foz the ſluttyſſhe
and fylthye marchandyſe of the
wozlde. He ſayth, *Niſi te cognoueris*   Cant. 1.
pulcherrima inter fœminas, O mooſte
feyzeſt amonge womenne, but if
thou knowe thy ſelfe. The ſpouſe
thzetteneth his virgins, oneleſſe
they wyll aknowlege theyz bleſ=
ſednes. But they aknowledge it
not, which repent, that they haue
bounde them ſelfes to liue a holy
chaſte lyfe, noz they whiche gape
and loke after wozldly vanities
and pleaſures. Calle vnto youre
remembzance, to whome you be
ſpowſed, and loue and ſtycke to
                      hym

hym with al your very hartes, in whom ones you haue al thynges the whiche are ioyfull and magnifycent. Let the example of the mooſte holy yonge men animate and courage you to be conſtant, the which ſhall a great deale the moꝛe reioyce ⁊ be glad, that their bodies as pledges be reſerued ⁊ kepte in your Colledge, yf they mowe perceyue, that you be folowers of thoſe theyꝛ vertues, with the which they pleaſed god. They oꝛnate and garnyſhe your religious company: ſoo in lyke maner ſe that you with integritie of lyfe and moſte pure and honeſte conuerſations hight them agayne. They chaſe rather to ſuffer many and dyuers kyndes of tourmentes and peynes, thenne they wolde ones taaſte hoggis fleſhe.

Loke

Loke that you repute ꝗ thynke it
to be hoggis flesshe, what so euer
is displesāt to your spouse. If you
wyll be emulaters and folowers
of this most goodly conflict, you
shall be part takers of theyr glo=
ry, by the helpe of your spouse
Chꝛist Jesu, whiche with
the father and the holy
gooste lyueth and
reygneth eter=
nally.
A M E N.

⁋Thus endeth the com=
paration of a vyꝛ=
gyne and a
Martyꝛ.

LONDINI IN AEDI-
BVS THOMAE BER-
THELETI RE-
GII IMPRES-
SORIS.
CVM PRIVILEGIO.